Dominic Bradbury

Photographs by
Richard Powers

Foreword by
Alain de Botton

The Iconic British House

Modern Architectural Masterworks Since 1900

CONTENTS

FOREWORD

Houses matter a lot. We are profoundly at their mercy. How we feel – our degree of hope, ambition, kindness, concentration and contentment – is dependent on such complex and expensive matters as the heights of the ceilings, the width of the windows and the artistry and talent behind the floorboards, curtains and banisters. Without good architecture, we cannot be properly or fully ourselves.

This leaves us in a tricky position because many houses are far from iconic. The title of this wonderful book contains both an open promise and a secret lamentation. That fifty lovely houses deserve a book all to themselves is in part a sign that the other 23.7 million or so other dwellings in the UK may not be worthy of this kind of interest.

It is a strange and surprising state of affairs. The goal of modern capitalism has long been to democratize and make readily available all that is good and worth having. This has worked extremely well when it comes to most consumer items: cars, televisions, phones, food and so on. And yet, crucially, houses are the exception. In the UK, it is as hard to find a delightful home today as it would have been to find a well-appointed bathroom in the twelfth century. Most of us are – still – *daydreaming* about good architecture rather than being able to set up home in an example of such a thing.

This book should leave us inspired and a little angry, in a fruitful way. Why can't everyone have access to the sort of high-quality housing on display here? Why aren't these sorts of jewels on offer everywhere? Why do we have to salivate over designs that should be part of our everyday lives? A common response on shutting the book may simply be: 'I want one!' That is a wholly legitimate aspiration, and a reaction that should incite us to ask more of property developers, government and architects.

The UK does have a hopeful story in this regard. In the great age of Georgian architecture, hundreds of thousands of near-identical homes were built across the country. They were elegant, functional, uplifting and – most importantly of all – affordable to many. There were a few so-called iconic houses, but the essence of the achievement of the Georgians was to devise standardized designs that could be rolled out in the hundreds of thousands.

Icons are extremely useful for galvanizing interest and framing ambition. We need to see what is possible in order to raise our collective sights. But icons should never remain one-off museum pieces. Their true destiny is to provide the models for the sort of mass-produced, standardized versions of the houses that we need for tomorrow. The team behind this beautiful book will have succeeded when, at last, the ordinary British house is as liveable, refined and inspiring as these sublime icons.

Alain de Botton

Designed by FAT Architecture and artist Grayson Perry, A House for Essex forms part of a collection of holiday rental homes known as Living Architecture, founded by Alain de Botton to provide guests with immersive experiences of modern design.

INTRODUCTION

Within a country where the theme of house and home is something of a national obsession, a spirit of adventure is threaded through the UK's residential architecture. The country's architects and designers have always played a powerful part in shaping the evolution of architectural ideas, while often drawing on tradition and vernacular influences, and this is certainly true in the twentieth and twenty-first centuries, a period in which the British home and the way that we live have been completely transformed.

Arts and Crafts architects, such as Edwin Lutyens (see p. 15), E. S. Prior (see p. 33) and Charles Voysey (see p. 39) were the precursors of a modern way of thinking about architecture, even as they looked to the past for inspiration and a pre-industrial approach to artisanal craftsmanship. They were, in their own way, turn-of-the-century innovators who experimented with new materials as well as old, while exploring fresh layouts and a more fluid approach to space than their predecessors. They began using concrete frameworks in conjunction with such natural materials as wood and stone, while reviving the idea of the 'great room' – a multifunctional and semi-open-plan space that was the heart of the Arts and Crafts home. Lutyens, Prior and others made use of butterfly plans, where the great room served as a link between the wings at either side, reaching out towards the light and the surroundings.

Scottish architect Charles Rennie Mackintosh (see p. 27) famously drew upon the Arts and Crafts tradition but also adopted decorative ideas and motifs associated with Art Nouveau, while referencing the Scottish vernacular and Japanese interiors. Mackintosh was one of the UK's most original voices of the early twentieth century, whose work was much admired on the continent and further afield.

Particularly between the world wars, British architecture and design were enriched by émigrés from Europe who encouraged this spirit of adventure. Berthold Lubetkin (see p. 45) and Ernő Goldfinger, among others, helped to pioneer and promote early Modernism in the UK, applying it to housing and residential design, and finding common ground with home-grown Modernists such as Oliver Hill (see p. 55) and Colin Lucas (see p. 73), who went into partnership with two incomers from New Zealand, Amyas Connell and Basil Ward. For a brief period, before they moved on to the USA, former Bauhaus masters from Germany, including Walter Gropius and Marcel Breuer, called the UK home. Even though their stay was short, these architects left their mark in many different ways, for example at Breuer's Sea Lane House on the West Sussex coast (see p. 61).

The progression of Modernism did not always run smoothly, however, as the battle over Colin Lucas's 66 Frognal in London suggested (see p. 73). In the 1930s, Lucas and his client,

Graham Phillips, Skywood House, 1999

solicitor Geoffrey Walford, found themselves involved in a series of bitter and public arguments with a number of older architects and traditionalists who felt that things had gone too far and the UK was beginning to embrace an imported style rather than finding its own way. The battle of 66 Frognal was a first salvo within a series of 'style wars' that were fought a number of times during the second half of the twentieth century.

The devastation caused by the bombing campaigns of World War II, particularly its impact upon British cities, was extreme and horrific, with the country taking many years to even begin to recover from life during wartime. But eventually, following the 1951 Festival of Britain, the UK started to rebuild and slowly reinvent itself. Despite the myth of sleepy conservatism, the 1950s and 1960s were a period

From left to right Oliver Hill, Cherry Hill, 1936; Berthold Lubetkin, Bungalow A, 1935; Jørn Utzon and Povl Ahm, The Ahm House, 1963; Meredith Bowles, The Black House, 2004; Team 4, Creek Vean, 1966; Foster Lomas, Sartfell Restorative Rural Retreat, 2019

of great originality in British architecture, with a golden wave of mid-century houses. They included architect Peter Womersley's High Sunderland in Selkirk, Scotland, designed for and in collaboration with celebrated textile designer Bernat Klein (see p. 79), and the house alongside the Beaulieu River that Basil Spence – whose long and varied career encompassed Arts and Crafts, Scandinavian-inspired Expressionism and high Brutalism – designed for himself and his family (see p. 97).

Brutalism – or more specifically New Brutalism – was born and defined in the UK during the 1960s, when critic Reyner Banham coined the term to describe the work of Alison and Peter Smithson (see p. 103). High Tech was another British construct, developed by such architects as Richard Rogers (see p. 133) and Michael Hopkins (see p. 151). Drawing a degree of inspiration from the American post-war model of steel-framed buildings and their curtain walls of glass, the High Tech architects pioneered a wave of buildings that were lightweight, super-efficient and semi-transparent and in which the highly engineered tectonic systems used

to create them were expressed and highlighted rather than hidden away. Postmodernism, too, flourished in the UK for a time, as seen in the work of Terry Farrell, who collaborated with architect, designer and critic Charles Jencks on a physical manifesto for the movement in the Cosmic House (see p. 157).

In the early decades of the twenty-first century, the work of British architects and designers has continued to have an international relevance and resonance. Consider David Chipperfield (see p. 231), Ken Shuttleworth (see p. 171) and others, along with a generation that has done so much to reinvigorate and reinterpret the grand tradition of the English country house and the British coastal retreat.

Increasingly, the style wars of the past have given way to a much more intelligent and sophisticated approach, which has seen various imaginative fusions of past and present, tradition and modernity. The Smithsons famously pioneered the idea of 'found space' with their own homes, including the Upper Lawn Pavilion in Wiltshire (see p. 103), which incorporated

parts of the ruined cottage that once stood on the same site. Increasingly, contemporary British architects have developed this approach, as seen in Witherford Watson Mann's Astley Castle in Warwickshire (see p. 237), or Lily Jencks's Ruins Studio in Dumfriesshire (see p. 267). Within these engaging residential escapes, the history of the past is woven into the fabric of a new home, echoing increasing calls for the adaptive reuse of existing buildings rather than continually opting for replacement. Adaptive reuse also forms part of the wider and essential theme of sustainability, which is explored in many of the later houses featured in the book.

For many years, there has been a continuing debate around whether there is a truly British architectural identity, especially when it comes to house and home. Back in the 1920s, Charles Voysey echoed Augustus Pugin (1812–1852) in calling for a uniquely British form of architecture, arguing that just as the UK has its own climate, geography and geology then surely it must have its own architectural identity. Writing in the introduction to Trevor Dannatt's (see p. 85) landmark 1959

book *Modern Architecture in Britain*, architectural historian John Summerson expressed similar sentiments while praising the fresh spirit of experimentalism across the country: 'There is now a real school of modern design in Great Britain,' he wrote. 'This agreement goes deeper than a sharing of stylistic conventions, which come and go fashionwise; it is an agreement to be radical.... This radicalism is the great thing in English architecture today.'

To my mind, the houses over the following pages suggest that there is, in broad terms, a unique identity to British architecture. In a similar way to our previous books, *The Iconic House* and *The Iconic American House*, we have sought to examine the most influential residences of the last 120 years or so authored by leading architects and designers, while exploring a range of stylistic and aesthetic movements as well as a wide range of settings, including – in this case – houses from England, Wales, Scotland and Northern Ireland. The majority of these projects are born of their particular contexts, drawing inspiration from the landscape and from the vernacular.

They reference the English country house tradition and that of follies floating in the landscape, along with the picturesque, as well as the intrinsic, characterful beauty of farmsteads and farm houses. Examples are Skene Catling de la Peña's Flint House in Buckinghamshire (see p. 255), James Gorst's Hannington Farm in Northamptonshire (see p. 291) and Adam Richards's Nithurst Farm in Sussex (see p. 285), all of which allude to the country's past while at the same time creating something modern, original and uniquely British.

There is, as with so many other countries, a worrying level of mediocrity when it comes to pattern-book residential and housing developments across the UK. Yet the depth and breadth of the architectural talent seen in this book, along with the solid foundations upon which it is built, gives rise to optimism that British architecture will continue to thrive while making a positive difference to the built environment around us, particularly when it comes to the precious subject of house and home.

GODDARDS
ABINGER COMMON, SURREY
Edwin Lutyens (1900)

Widely regarded as one of Edwin Lutyens's most inventive and original residential projects, Goddards was born of a generous act of philanthropy. The architect's clients were wealthy entrepreneur Frederick James Mirrielees (1851–1914) and his wife Margaret, a shipping-line heiress, who wanted to build a rest home for 'ladies of small means', such as nurses and governesses. The original idea for Goddards was that it would be used only in the summer months and would offer amenities for both rest and recreation, including gardens and grounds masterminded by renowned landscape designer Gertrude Jekyll (1843–1942). It was Jekyll, who Lutyens (1869–1944) knew well and collaborated with on many occasions, who introduced the architect to the clients.

The combination of these generous clients and a relatively open brief allowed Lutyens a good deal of latitude in creating a unique rural retreat on the 7-acre site near Abinger Common. In many respects, Goddards was ambitious and innovative, yet the nature of the project meant that it was well suited to an almost monastic level of simplicity within, instead of the more layered and luxurious spaces that the architect's clients usually required. The programme, therefore, complemented an Arts and Crafts aesthetic that referenced the purity of medieval manor houses and the values of the pre-industrial age.

The Mirrielees family had originally anticipated two cottages that would share a more generous communal space, but were also open minded and willing to invest in the project to make it a success. Lutyens's solution was to develop an innovative butterfly plan for the two-storey house, with two distinct splayed wings tied together by a spacious great room, modelled upon a medieval hall, situated on the ground floor at the centre of the design. Doubling as a hallway and circulation link, this common room featured a large fireplace at one end, wooden floors, exposed ceiling trusses and beams, and had room enough for a long dining table and additional seating around the edges.

A kitchen and service spaces sat in one wing while the other was dominated by an indoor skittle alley, with brick arches

Below The inglenook fireplace in the great room, with its integrated window seat, is a familiar emblem of the Arts and Crafts home.

Opposite The choice of materials such as timber, tiles and stone sits well with the Arts and Crafts ethos, while integrated elements – niches, cupboards and alcoves – suggest the attention to detail exhibited throughout.

supporting the vaulted ceiling, providing a tempting games room that could be used in any weather. Upstairs, the servants' rooms were at the centre, above the great hall, while each wing had three bedrooms for visiting residents. Given that the house was for summer use, there was minimal attention in the initial design to bathing and bathrooms. As well as brick and stone, materials included clay tiles for the roof, lime-washed plaster walls and extensive timber joinery within. The original furniture comprised a sympathetic choice of pieces by the Art Workers' Guild.

Lutyens visited Goddards soon after its completion, enjoying a game of skittles in the indoor alley: 'It seems very successful and the intimates love it and invariably weep when they leave it, which is comforting. Mirrielees seems very happy with it too.'[1]

Some years later, in 1910, Lutyens was asked to return once again and extend the house. The Mirrielees family had decided to relocate the rest home and convert Goddards into a private home for the couple's son, Donald Mirrielees, and his wife. The butterfly plan allowed Lutyens to add a new library to one

Opposite An amenity to be enjoyed in all weather, the indoor skittle alley is one of the glories of this escapist retreat, with its vaulted brick arches and long ribbon of windows drawing in sunlight and framing the gardens.

Below Although the retreat has been updated, not least by Lutyens himself, the bedrooms and bathrooms retain a sense of simplicity while seeking links with the semi-rural setting.

wing and a new dining room to the other, along with a further two bedrooms upstairs, without disturbing the character of the house, while more luxurious bathrooms were also provided. Such a formation, which was to prove popular among other Arts and Crafts designers such as E. S. Prior (see p. 33), also maximized access to light and connections with the surrounding gardens.

The house and gardens are now under the guardianship of the Lutyens Trust and the Landmark Trust, which have fully restored Goddards. The house, with the exception of the library, is now available for holiday rental and sleeps up to twelve guests. Continuing to serve as a rural retreat for visitors, it feels as though the house has – in a way – come full circle.

BLACKWELL
BOWNESS-ON-WINDERMERE, CUMBRIA
M. H. Baillie Scott (1900)

Opposite The house enjoys a prominent hillside position looking over Bowness towards Lake Windermere and the wooded countryside on its opposite shore.

Above The elegant detailing of windows and chimneys adds to the engaging character of Blackwell, while the orientation of the house responds not only to the views but also to its immediate surroundings.

Arts and Crafts master Mackay Hugh Baillie Scott (1865–1945) was one of the most successful British architects of his generation. Around the turn of the century, his work was much in demand not only in his home country but also in Europe, where he was commissioned by the Grand Duke of Hesse, Ernst Ludwig, to work on the interiors of his home in Darmstadt during the late 1890s, with other residential projects following in Switzerland, France and Austria. His most famous house in England is Blackwell, on the edge of Lake Windermere, which – like so much of his work – refers back to a golden age of craftsmanship while also incorporating modern services and technology, including electric lighting, central heating and free-flowing living spaces.

The house was commissioned by a wealthy industrialist and brewery owner named Edward Holt (1849–1928) for use as a summer retreat for himself, his wife Elizabeth and their children. Holt served two terms as Lord Mayor of Manchester and was instrumental in bringing fresh water to the city via new reservoirs in the Lake District. Here, he also found a sublime hillside site looking out over Bowness-on-Windermere and across the lake itself.

The setting, within an area that had become highly sought after during the late nineteenth century, was certainly inspirational. Baillie Scott tied the substantial, three-storey family home to its site using local stone and slate, while the grounds were laid out by Thomas Mawson (1861–1933), a landscape designer based in the region but with a national reputation. Baillie Scott decided upon an L-shaped plan, with the principal rooms facing southwards while service spaces, as well as the main entrance, are positioned towards the north.

The main hall, or great room, sits at the centre of the plan. A generously scaled room, it is suited to entertaining, complete with an inglenook fireplace with integrated benches to either side, as well as other familiar Arts and Crafts reference points, including a Tudor-esque minstrel's gallery and the repeated use of motifs and symbols drawn from the natural world. A dining room is situated on one side of this pivotal space, while on the other sits the white drawing room. This is undoubtedly one of the

Opposite The interiors of the great room feature multiple references to the natural world, seen both in the wooden panelling and the decorative frieze between the panels and the exposed ceiling beams.

Below The focal point of the great room is the inglenook fireplace and integrated seating, which forms a room within a room, topped by a mezzanine gallery; the separate dining room alongside is a more intimately scaled space with an organic warmth drawn from the use of natural materials, tones and textures.

most enticing rooms in the property, with its own inglenook and a bay window that offers some of the best views from the house, but with – as the name suggests – a lighter palette than the other key living spaces: ornate white plasterwork on the walls and ceilings contrasts with the wooden floors. Upstairs, the principal family bedrooms have lake views best enjoyed from the window seats. The attic level was devoted to the servants' quarters.

It is the cohesive fusion of architectural and interior design that makes Blackwell so special, and won Baillie Scott many admirers. The house is included in Hermann Muthesius' landmark book, *The English House*, first published in 1904, with the author praising Blackwell and its interiors as 'an autonomous work of art':

The house combines dignity with great comfort and a poetical atmosphere within…. The drawing-room is white throughout, with delicate relief decoration on the frieze and ceiling. The other rooms are all designed down to the last detail in the same careful manner, so that the house may be regarded as one of the most attractive creations that the new movement in house-building has produced.[2]

Fully restored in 2001 and opened to the public, Blackwell is still regarded as one of the great country houses of the Lake District and one of its most influential, alongside John Ruskin's Brantwood on Lake Coniston.

Below The white drawing room is one of the most inviting spaces at Blackwell, with its beautifully crafted fireplace, window seat and fitted bookcases woven into one cohesive design.

Right The generously scaled bay window in the white drawing room overlooks the grounds of the house. Its integrated window seat is one of the many elements that add to the sophisticated fusion of architecture and interior design.

An able self-publicist, Baillie Scott included the house in magazines such as *The Studio* and his own book, *Houses & Gardens* (1906), adding to his growing reputation.

HILL HOUSE
HELENSBURGH, ARGYLL AND BUTE
Charles Rennie Mackintosh (1904)

Scottish architect and designer Charles Rennie Mackintosh (1868–1928) developed an aesthetic approach that was truly original and instantly recognizable. It was a design philosophy of convergence, which drew upon ideas and ingredients from Art Nouveau, Arts and Crafts and the Scottish vernacular, as well as inspiration from Japan and other parts of the world. His most important work was undertaken at the turning point of two centuries and looked both to the past and to the future. At the same time, Mackintosh was an artist with a unique style of his own. All of these elements came together and were expressed to the full with the invention of Hill House in Helensburgh.

During the earliest years of the twentieth century Mackintosh was a young architect who had already found fame as the designer of the first phase of the Glasgow School of Art (1899), as well as collaborating on interiors with his wife, artist Margaret Macdonald Mackintosh (1864–1933). This was a time of intense creativity for them both, with commissions including the Willow Tearooms in Glasgow for patron Catherine Cranston and Mackintosh's first private house, Windyhill, at Kilmacolm to the west of Glasgow, completed in 1901.

Mackintosh was recommended to publisher Walter Blackie by Blackie & Son's art director, Talwin Morris. Blackie, whose offices were in Glasgow, and his wife Anna were looking for a new home for their family and planned to move from Dunblane to Helensburgh, a desirable town on the northern shore of the Firth of Clyde and within easy reach of the city by train. They found a hillside site on the edge of the town and approached Mackintosh. Blackie recalled:

> When he entered my room I was astonished at the youthfulness of the distinguished architect.... I told him that I disliked red-tiled roofs in the West of Scotland, with its frequent murky sky; did not want to have a construction of brick and plaster and wooden beams; that, on the whole, I rather fancied grey rough cast for the walls, and slate for the roof, and that any architectural effect sought should be secured by the massing of the parts rather than by adventitious ornament.[3]

Opposite The architecture of Hill House references the Scottish baronial tradition, with rough-cast walls and a slate roof, but also introduces a modern level of abstraction.

Above There is a cubist quality to the exterior of the house, with Mackintosh's original combination of components – including the chimneys and fenestration – creating a fresh interpretation of the Scottish country house.

Above The interiors of Hill House are a collaboration between Mackintosh and his wife, artist Margaret Macdonald Mackintosh, creating a total work of art covering every design element of the family home.

Opposite Furniture, textiles, lighting and decorative motifs are all part of the couple's cohesive vision for the house, fusing Art Nouveau, Arts and Crafts and vernacular references. Features such as the conning tower stairway can be seen as precursors of Modernist architecture and designs.

Mackintosh did his best to oblige. Having taken the Blackies to visit Windyhill, the architect won the commission for a generously scaled house with space enough for a family with five children and house staff. The resulting home was arranged over three storeys, including an attic level with servants' quarters and a schoolroom.

Externally, the architecture of Hill House borrows from the Scottish tradition of grand baronial residences and castles. Yet the level of abstraction seen in various parts of the design, such as the semi-cylindrical staircase, gives the house an almost sculptural or cubist quality that is distinctly modern in feel.

Internally, Mackintosh and his wife collaborated on every detail and incorporated gas lighting in the bespoke lanterns and luxurious bathrooms. The principal living spaces sit at the centre of the ground-floor plan, with the Mackintoshs designing many integrated elements throughout, such as the elegantly crafted fireplaces and window seats, as well as loose pieces of furniture, carpets and textiles. A library is situated to one side of these principal spaces and was to have been joined by a billiard room that was dropped at the last minute. On the other side is a series of service spaces. The family bedrooms,

Above The commitment to bespoke furniture and detailing carries through to the family's private realm, as seen in the bed and headboard framed by the vaulted ceiling, while the bathrooms incorporate multiple modern luxuries.

Opposite Floral motifs and references to nature characterize the distinctive approach to interior decoration and the 'Glasgow Style', as seen in the wall stencils, curtains and textiles.

nurseries and bathrooms are found at mid-level, with great thought given to storage spaces and fitted cupboards throughout, as well as to the decorative flourishes and motifs that enliven the interiors, with inspiration drawn repeatedly from flora and fauna.

Hill House was both functional and romantic, thoughtful and poetic. It has been compared with the work of Charles Voysey (see p. 39) and M. H. Baillie Scott (see p. 21), yet Mackintosh and his wife brought so many additional layers of meaning to the project. Their pioneering work on the cusp of modernity was much praised on the continent and by commentators ranging from Hermann Muthesius to Nikolaus Pevsner. Yet, after the

completion of the second phase of the Glasgow School of Art in 1909 followed by a move to London and Suffolk, Mackintosh's career began to falter.

Now owned by the National Trust for Scotland, who have been working on a substantial renovation programme, Hill House remains a much-loved monument to the 'Glasgow Style', expressed on a welcoming, residential scale.

VOEWOOD

HOLT, NORFOLK

E. S. Prior (1905)

English architect Edward Prior (1852–1932) adopted an increasingly contextual and organic approach as he stepped into the twentieth century. He emerged from an Arts and Crafts tradition, after working for many years with Norman Shaw (1831–1912), and was an expert in Gothic architecture, having published a landmark book on the subject in 1900. These early influences never left him, yet Prior became increasingly interested in modern building techniques and the idea that a house should not only be conditioned by the needs of its residents but also by the local experience of construction. The most complete expression of these concerns came in the form of Voewood in Norfolk, completed in 1905.

Situated on the green edges of Holt and a few miles from the North Norfolk coast, Voewood was commissioned by the Reverend Percy Lloyd (1868–1937) for himself and his wife, who was in poor health. It was felt that a rural retreat blessed with fresh breezes spilling in from the sea might be of benefit, and the provision of integrated solariums, or 'cloisters', formed part of the brief.

Prior decided to adopt a butterfly plan for Voewood, an X-shaped formation that allowed all parts of the house to make the most of the light and the views. The butterfly plan was successfully pioneered by such Arts and Crafts architects as Edwin Lutyens at Goddards (see p. 15), and it had already been used by Prior to great effect at a country house known as The Barn in Exmouth, Devon, completed in 1897.

The architect also decided to use a combination of an innovative concrete structural framework for the house along with local materials, particularly flint and brick. In keeping with his ideas about tying buildings to their site and setting, Prior excavated the grounds directly in front of the house to the south, collecting aggregates for the concrete and other raw materials, such as flint, for building the new house. This created a formal sunken garden, with steps ascending towards the terraces that sat alongside the solariums and the great hall situated at the centre of the butterfly plan. Voewood, or Home Place as it was also known, was then coated in flint punctuated with brickwork, including the

Opposite Voewood makes the most of natural and traditional materials, particularly local flint, but the framework of the house is made from reinforced concrete.

Above The sunken gardens at the front of the house were excavated to source the flint and aggregates for mixing the concrete that comprised some of the building materials for the butterfly house.

Below The main entrance is situated at one end of the building and steps up to the principal circulation route through the house, with the living room visible through the open doorway.

Opposite The great room, with its communal fireplace, sits at the heart of the butterfly plan; the main staircase leads up to a landing that becomes a mezzanine gallery overlooking the great room and linking the bedrooms in the two opposite wings of the house.

tall spiralling chimneys, along with terracotta tiles from Cambridgeshire for the roof.

Internally, the entrance hallway led towards a double-height great hall at the centre of the house, complete with an inglenook fireplace and Dutch tiles around the hearth; early photographs show a vast tapestry hanging over the inglenook and rugs laid on the wooden floors. A mezzanine gallery spans the hall while providing a landing linking the bedrooms situated within the two wings on the floors above.

The use of local materials and the ample provision of terraces and garden rooms allowed Prior to fully integrate the house and garden, as was his ambition. Voewood is widely regarded as Prior's residential masterpiece, where all of his influences fuse in one rounded and cohesive vision. Nonetheless, despite this and the significant cost of the project, the Lloyds themselves barely used the house. Shortly after completion, the house was let to another cleric, the Reverend Meyrick Jones, and then served as a school up until World War I. For much

Above The dining room and adjoining kitchen sit in the opposite wing of the house to the main entrance and living room, offering views over the gardens; here, as in the other principal rooms, the fireplace is the focal point.

Opposite This garden room was once open sided with a more direct sense of connection to the adjoining terrace and sunken gardens; later, it was more fully enclosed to create a light-filled solarium.

of the twentieth century the house became a convalescent home and was institutionalized over the years until eventually, in 1998, rare book dealer Simon Finch acquired Voewood and turned it back into a home. He also opened the property as a venue for weddings and special events.

Following Voewood, Prior worked on a small number of private houses, as well as churches including St Andrew's in Roker, Sunderland. But increasingly he switched his attention to education and was a pivotal figure in the establishment of the School of Architecture at the University of Cambridge, where he became

a professor in 1912 and devised the syllabus and a research programme, which included studies of modern construction techniques.

THE HOMESTEAD
FRINTON-ON-SEA, ESSEX
Charles Voysey (1906)

Opposite The L-shaped house sits on a corner plot and wraps its way around the rear garden, ensuring privacy for its terraces and lawn.

Above Stone, timber, brick and slate comprise the main ingredients within the palette of materials, with the lead gutters forming another bespoke element.

As well as being one of the most original and influential architects of the Arts and Crafts era, Charles Voysey (1857–1941) was also one of the most prolific. Compared with his close contemporaries, such as his friend and St John's Wood neighbour E. S. Prior (see p. 33), Voysey achieved particular success in applying Arts and Crafts principles to the design of smaller country retreats and suburban homes, as he sought to establish a truly English aesthetic style that took account of the context and local materials, as well as artisanal craftsmanship and order.

Voysey suggested that 'simplicity, sincerity, repose, directness and frankness are moral qualities as essential to good architecture as to good men',[4] and certainly there was a natural sense of discipline, rigour and functionality to his houses, with every detail carefully considered. There was an innate suspicion not only of machine-made goods and furniture, but also of the clumsiness of early domestic technology, such as central-heating systems, which Voysey worried would spoil the clarity of his rooms and spaces. Yet there was a progressive attitude to spatial planning and

the circulation of his homes, as well as a mastery of natural light and ventilation, that saw Voysey widely praised as an early pioneer of a modern approach to architecture. As seen in his wallpaper collections, there was also a playful side to Voysey's work that endeared him to clients, and pattern and decorative details found their way into his interiors.

Such themes were explored within the design of Voysey's own home, The Orchard, in Chorleywood, Hertfordshire, completed in 1899, where the architect and designer characteristically worked on every detail of the architecture and interiors, including the furniture. The same was true, a few years later, of The Homestead, in Frinton-on-Sea, which is of a comparable scale and design to The Orchard.

The client for The Homestead was Sydney Claridge Turner, a single gentleman who was the manager of a London-based insurance company. One of Turner's greatest passions was playing golf, which attracted him to the fast-growing community of Frinton-on-Sea where he was able to acquire a building plot almost alongside the golf course and only a short walk from the

esplanade and the seashore. His two-storey home was one of the first to be completed there.

Voysey embraced the corner plot by adopting an L-shaped plan, which helped to protect and shelter the rear garden, while existing trees towards the boundary were preserved. As with The Orchard, the architect used brick construction, coated in white render, along with stonework for the window frames and slate tiles for the roof. A heart-shaped letter box graced the arched front door, which led into the entrance hall and stairway at the crux of the L-shaped layout. To one side was an enfilade of service spaces, including the pantry, kitchen and scullery, while the other direction led to the dining room and then the great room, or parlour. This spacious retreat had an inglenook fireplace to one side, an integrated verandah to the other and a porthole window on the southeastern

Left The sitting room is arranged around the inglenook fireplace, with its tiled surround, while at the far end the porthole window over the piano faces in the direction of the sea.

Below The provision of angled doors and fitted cupboards in the dining room creates an octagonal space with a more intimate and enveloping character.

Below Bespoke joinery is threaded through the house, seen in features such as the doors with their wooden hinges, as well as the staircase and banisters.

Opposite Arches formed from fanned terracotta tiles are repeated motifs, seen in the kitchen downstairs but also in some of the bedrooms, where the archway frames the fireplace and softens this otherwise largely linear space.

corner pointing towards the sea. Upstairs, Voysey provided a handful of bedrooms with their own fireplaces and a bathroom.

Apart from the select use of cement floors for the service areas, the palette of materials comprised stone, tiles and timber floors. Here, as with The Orchard, great attention was paid to the details, from the design of the lead gutters to the wooden door latches and the half-height timber panelling in the dining room, as well as the fitted cupboards and doors that create an octagonal shape for this space for the evenings and entertaining. Voysey also incorporated a design for the rear garden, featuring a pergola, flower beds and, in the far corner, a rose garden.

BUNGALOW A
WHIPSNADE, BEDFORDSHIRE
Berthold Lubetkin (1935)

Opposite The composition of the Whipsnade dacha includes various curvaceous elements that soften and enrich the cabin, while contrasting with more linear ingredients such as the ribbon windows.

Above The design of the house makes the most of its setting, with mature trees offering a verdant backdrop to the bungalow and the main living spaces oriented towards the open views over the valley.

'When one is one's own client one can sing one's own song,' said pioneering Modernist Berthold Lubetkin (1901–1990).[5] During the 1930s, the architect welcomed the opportunity to design homes for himself and his family twice over. There was Berthold and Margaret Lubetkin's penthouse at Highpoint II in Highgate (1938), where they made the most of one of the engaging and generously scaled apartments in this landmark development. And there was Bungalow A, alongside Whipsnade Zoo, where Lubetkin embraced the hillside location and panoramic view, designing a modern version of a country cabin that offered a true rural retreat.

Along with Serge Chermayeff (1900–1996) and Ernő Goldfinger (1902–1987), Lubetkin was one of a number of émigré architects from Eastern Europe who settled in the UK between the world wars. Born in Georgia, he worked in Paris with Auguste Perret (1874–1954) after completing his studies and was then drawn to England, in 1931, by the promise of a commission to design a house. The commission never materialized but Lubtekin stayed on, founding the innovative architectural unit Tecton, while recognizing the possibility of making a significant contribution to the evolution of Modernism in the UK, particularly in terms of reinforced-concrete construction. Highpoint I (1935) and Highpoint II allowed Lubetkin to express his belief that Modern architecture could change people's lives for the better, with two apartment buildings featuring a range of progressive designs.

Another key strand of Tecton's work of the 1930s was for the Zoological Society of London (ZSL), beginning with the Gorilla House (1933) at London Zoo and soon after the iconic Penguin Pool (1934) and other projects at both London Zoo and the ZSL's Whipsnade Zoo near Dunstable, which opened in 1931 and was the first open-air zoological park in the world. Chief among Lubetkin's Whipsnade buildings was the Elephant House of 1935, the year in which he also completed his own dacha nearby (Bungalow A), as well as a second bungalow (Bungalow B, or 'Holly Frindle') for eye specialist Dr Ida Mann.

The ZSL provided Lubetkin and Ida Mann (1893–1983) with a modest site on the edge of Dunstable Downs, with open views from the bluff of the hill across the Bedfordshire plains.

Above Semi-sheltered terraces and suntraps are woven into the design of the dacha, with integrated planting also enlivening the sequence of outdoor rooms.

Opposite The partially shaded and sheltered porch at the front of the house frames the open vista of the valley, while the outdoor fireplace means that the verandah can also be used during the winter months.

Lubetkin seized the chance to explore new ideas, developing a plan for a T-shaped, single-storey building constructed with a system of reinforced-concrete panels, insulated with layers of cork, and ribbons of 'Thermolux' glass set within this structural framework.

He decided to lift the building slightly above ground level on a series of discreet pilings, with the resulting shadow gap, or 'flashgap', giving the bungalow a degree of lightness. Combined with the T-shaped layout, this act of levitation suggested, as Lubetkin put it, the 'significance of a glider at the point of take-off'.[6] A loggia at the front of the house, complete with an outdoor fireplace, offers a semi-sheltered space for enjoying the vista. A more enclosed courtyard to one side has a semicircular wall that softens the linear outline of the building. Lubetkin made playful use of vivid colours at key points to contrast with the white rendered walls, as well as repeated architectural motifs, for example the use of circular glass bricks embedded in the boundary walls and part of the loggia's canopy.

Inside, he designed a spacious, open-plan living room with an adjoining dining room, and a separate, compact kitchen. Another curvaceous partition separates this part of the house from the two bedrooms and a bathroom at the rear.

Lubetkin continued to win major commissions during the late 1930s before retreating from his profession during the post-war period. More recently, both bungalows have been restored by architect Mike Davies of Rogers Stirk Harbour + Partners.

DORCHESTER DRIVE
HERNE HILL, LONDON
Kemp & Tasker (1936)

Architects Leslie Kemp (1899–1997) and Frederick Tasker were best known for a series of Art Deco cinemas built in and around London during the 1930s. But they were also involved in the design and build of a number of pioneering residential projects, such as the creation of a prototypical house of the future designed for the 'Village of Tomorrow' at the 1934 Ideal Home Show. At around the same time they were designing this inventive and original villa in Herne Hill, which is a showcase of sophisticated Deco style.

Kemp & Tasker's client was a property developer and house builder called H. C. Morrell, who made a significant impact on the south London suburb. Morrell built a Deco block of flats here, known as Dorchester Court, and helped to establish Temple Bowling Club. He also built two houses nearby, one for his mother and his own family home, which took luxurious modern living to a new level.

This three-storey house with a cubist outline sits in generous grounds, and has an integrated verandah forming an outdoor room overlooking the back garden, supplemented by roof terraces on two levels. The house is built principally of brick and has substantial steel-framed windows and a balcony over the front entrance, where mosaics on the steps and celadon tilework around the doorway hint at the level of thought and detailing running through the design.

Inside, two of the greatest delights are the entrance hall and staircase. An angled fireplace offers a warm welcome, while materials include parquet for the floors and ornate ironwork for the staircase balustrade, which winds its way up to a half landing by the balcony window over the doorway, drawing sunlight into this suitably dramatic space. As elsewhere, every detail is a bespoke design by Kemp & Tasker, from the banisters and door handles to the light switches. The generous drawing room off the hallway incorporates a seating area arranged around a Deco fireplace and a streamlined cornice, while windows and French doors connect this key space to the verandah and the back garden. Originally, the house had a billiard room, complete with a bespoke table and scoreboard.

Upstairs, the sense of theatre continues in the master bedroom and bathroom. The bedroom features a gas fireplace with a marble

Opposite The front door leads into a light-filled hallway with a parquet floor and custom detailing, while the staircase runs up and around this welcoming space.

Above As well as the fireplace, the sitting room features Art Deco details such as the cornicing, while the French windows lead to a loggia facing the rear garden.

border and an illuminated surround, while the bathroom has a state-of-the-art power shower and a sunken bath with a marble surround and gold taps. Panelling and the vanity unit are made from onyx and the walls are mirrored throughout; the lighting here is also integrated and even the shower head is illuminated.

More recently the house was acquired by architectural designer Mike Rundell, who began a renovation and modernization programme. Rundell was greatly assisted by the fact that the two previous owners had carefully preserved so much of the original detailing and had left the layout largely unaltered. The only area that had

seen substantial change was the kitchen, which Rundell redesigned in an appropriate style while introducing twenty-first-century amenities. He also sourced or designed a sympathetic set of furniture for the house. He explains:

It was designed as a practical and elegant family home so I wanted to preserve it as such…. There are very few intact examples of private, bespoke Art Deco design in the UK. Eltham Palace is similar in atmosphere, but considerably larger in scale, while other examples are usually heavily restored. This house is truly original.

Opposite Apart from the new kitchen, which was redesigned in a sympathetic style, the majority of the luxurious features in the bathrooms, dressing rooms and elsewhere are original to the house.

Above The master bathroom is one of the most theatrical spaces in the house, with its use of marble, mirrored glass, integrated lighting fixtures and golden details such as the taps and spout.

CHERRY HILL
WENTWORTH ESTATE, SURREY
Oliver Hill (1936)

Opposite The architecture and landscape design of Cherry Hill work hand in hand, with the mature trees forming a verdant backdrop to the crisply rendered house.

Above With its streamlined Deco curves and terraces, the residence references ocean liners and machine-age living with a focus on modern luxuries throughout.

Perched on the leafy edge of Wentworth golf course, Cherry Hill is the most ambitious and luxurious of the early Modernist houses designed by English architect Oliver Hill (1887–1968). Originally known as Holthanger, the house exhibits Hill's love of streamlining, with sinuous curves and elegant finishes that help lift the character of the building and set it apart from the more linear designs adopted by many of his contemporaries. There is a subtle ocean-liner influence, not only in the more curvaceous elements of Cherry Hill but also in the fenestration, the decks and terraces around the house, and the level of finish and detailing seen in the recently restored and updated residence.

Many of Hill's early residential projects of the 1920s adopted an Arts and Crafts ethos, with the influence of his mentor Edwin Lutyens particularly evident. But in 1930 Hill visited the Stockholm Exhibition, where he noted the work of architect Gunnar Asplund (1885–1940) and others who had shifted decidedly towards Modernism while still retaining their respect for the past. His projects of the early 1930s

suggested this fresh direction, drawing upon Modernist principles yet also exhibiting a fondness for streamlined Art Deco lines and fine materials.

Two of Hill's key projects from the early 1930s share certain similarities with Cherry Hill. The first, a house called Joldwynds in Holmsbury St Mary in Surrey (1932), uses eye-catching cylindrical elements such as the staircase to soften the outline of the building and to bring an exuberant and expressive quality to the home. The same was true of the LMS Midland Hotel in Morecambe in Lancashire (1933), where Hill made the most of the seaside location to create a sculptural building complete with a circular café and restaurant at one end.

Cherry Hill adopted a number of motifs and devices from these earlier projects, but within an enticing, semi-rural context where the architect was also able to indulge his interest in landscape design and interiors to create a rounded and contextual home. The driveway, approach and entrance were designed around the mature pine trees on the site, including two trees that flanked the main entrance and which

Opposite The cylindrical stairway at the front of the house also serves as a way of drawing sunlight deep into the building via its curvaceous walls of glass, while framing views of the grounds.

Below The sequence of living spaces overlooking the rear garden creates a vibrant 'promenade architecturale' leading towards the solarium and adjoining terraces.

have been reinstated in the recent restoration by Tejit and Jess Bath, in association with John Allan of Avanti Architects.

A glass-fronted cylindrical staircase at night becomes a dramatic lantern adjacent to the front door of the two storey-home, echoed by a circular water tower on the roof. The gently curving brick walls of the building are rendered and painted white, lending the house a crisp, sculptural outline. The main living spaces are arranged in a fluid line towards the rear of the house, overlooking the terraces and the sunken

garden. The semicircular sun room, in particular, offers a vivid sense of connection with the grounds, while the golf course lies just beyond the tree line.

Hill's original client was Katherine Hannah Newton, whose family were wealthy industrialists. Soon after completion, the house featured in a 1937 exhibition at the Museum of Modern Art (MoMA) in New York entitled 'Modern Architecture in England'. In 1958, the house was bought by John Hay Whitney, American ambassador to the UK, who was also

an investor and philanthropist. Whitney and his wife Betsey renamed it Cherry Hill after a Denver country club where the ambassador enjoyed playing golf with President Eisenhower. The easy proximity to Wentworth golf course, as well as to Ascot, all added to the appeal of the house for them. The Whitneys used Cherry Hill for entertaining, while layering the walls with their extraordinary art collection, which focused on the French Impressionists.

The recent renovation of the house takes inspiration from the thirty-year period when the Whitneys owned the house, with the idea of creating an equally luxurious home but with the benefit of twenty-first-century services and amenities. Allan replaced inappropriate extensions from the post-Whitney period with fresh, sympathetic additions while original features have been preserved and restored throughout the listed house. The gardens have also been revived in a considerate manner, respecting the mature trees that still encircle the property and enhance the sense of seclusion.

Above The house has been sensitively updated and gently extended by architect John Allan, much respected for his work in the conservation and revival of Modernist buildings.

Opposite The solarium overlooks the sunken gardens to the rear of the property but also connects with the terraces and decks, which provide tempting summertime spaces.

SEA LANE HOUSE
ANGMERING-ON-SEA, WEST SUSSEX
Marcel Breuer (1936)

Although the former Bauhaus master Marcel Breuer (1902–1981) spent just two years in the UK, he managed to achieve a great deal. The Hungarian-born architect and designer followed his friend and mentor Walter Gropius (1883–1969) to the UK in 1935 and formed a working partnership with the London-based architect F. R. S. Yorke (1906–1962). Despite an initially limited command of the English language, Breuer was able to advance his innovative and influential work in the field of furniture design through a new collection of plywood and laminate pieces produced by Jack Pritchard's (1899–1992) Isokon. At the same time, Breuer worked on a handful of architectural and interiors commissions that have been described as the 'missing link' between his early work in Europe and his mature period following on from his arrival in the USA in 1937.

Breuer's British portfolio included a temporary pavilion, which he once described as one of his favourite buildings, at the Royal West of England Show for another furniture producer, Crofton Gane (1877–1967). The Gane Pavilion of 1936 was a modestly sized,

single-storey building of glass, wood and stone with the character of a rounded home, allowing the company's furniture to be displayed in a domestic setting. Inevitably, the Pavilion was taken down after the show, and other Breuer projects of the period were substantially altered or replaced. The only known surviving Marcel Breuer house is, therefore, Sea Lane House on the West Sussex coast.

Breuer's client was a bandleader, James Macnabb, who approached the architect and F. R. S. Yorke in the summer of 1936. The site itself is around 70 m from the sea but is flanked by neighbouring houses, which have increased in number over the years. Breuer decided to lift the house upwards on a series of piloti so that the main living spaces would still be able to enjoy views of the sea over the top of the adjacent buildings and nearby trees.

Initially, Breuer designed a three-storey house but objections to the plans from neighbours and the local authority focused on the height of the house, particularly as most other homes in the surrounding village were one or two storeys. Breuer significantly amended

the design to create a house on two levels and with two distinct wings, arranged in an L-shaped formation.

The ground floor holds the main entrance, kitchen, pantry and ancillary spaces, as well as a covered garage and an open car port under one of the floating wings, which also serves as a semi-sheltered verandah. Heading upstairs, the dining area and living room feature substantial windows looking out to the coast but also leading out onto a curvaceous, floating terrace, which helps soften the otherwise linear outline of the building while also connecting with an external staircase for a more immediate link to the garden. The bedroom wing projects outwards into the garden and towards the sea, with a neat line of family bedrooms linked by

a landing to one side. Originally, this line included six bedrooms and one bathroom.

The house itself was built out of brick, with concrete structural elements and supports. The brickwork was initially painted white and later rendered to create a smooth, crisp coat, yet the feeling of lightness was preserved with the idea of a floating building raised up above the garden. The positioning of the house to take best advantage of its viewpoint over the coast meant that it was adopted as a gun emplacement during the war, after which it was sold to new owners.

It seems unclear whether or not Breuer ever saw the completed house, as he left for the USA in 1937 just before it was finished. After settling in the USA, Breuer adapted

his thinking to fresh contexts, developing a sequence of American houses and gradually progressing to projects of a larger scale, including the Whitney Museum of American Art (1966), as well as returning to Europe for commissions such as the UNESCO Headquarters in Paris (1958) and the French alpine ski resort of Flaine, begun in 1960 and completed in 1976.

Above The bedrooms and bathrooms run within a linear sequence over the length of the elevated sleeping wing; fitted furniture and storage in various parts of the house are part of the original design.

Opposite The curvaceous balcony and terrace at the front of the house soften an otherwise linear composition, with its wave-like form sitting well with the coastal context.

ELTHAM PALACE

ELTHAM, LONDON
Seely & Paget (1936)

Opposite The Courtaulds' mansion sits among the remnants and ruins of the old Tudor palace, with the former great hall woven into the V-shaped plan.

Above The architecture and interiors fuse a neo-classical 'Wrenaissance' approach with streamlined Art Deco interiors, resulting in a combination that ensures a sense of opulent grandeur throughout.

During the 1930s, Stephen (1883–1967) and Virginia (1883–1972) Courtauld were one of the most glamorous and intriguing couples in London, with a truly palatial home. Their lives were full of adventure, with their marriage said to have prospered despite – or perhaps on account of – their contrasting personalities, with one of the two rather serious and reserved (Stephen) and the other outgoing with a love of entertaining (Virginia). They created a series of extraordinary houses for themselves in France and Rhodesia, but it was Eltham Palace that was their most illustrious home.

Stephen was part of the Courtauld textile family yet never joined the family business, preferring to use his wealth to pursue other interests. Having won the Military Cross for his distinguished service during World War I, he became a member of the first mountaineering team to successfully scale the Innominata face of Mont Blanc. Later, as a leading light of the Royal Geographical Society, Courtauld helped to fund and organize the British Arctic Air Route Expedition of 1930 to 1931. He also helped to launch the Ealing film studios in

West London and supported a range of other artistic and educational causes.

Virginia, who met her future husband in the Italian Alps, came from a very different background. Born in Romania, she was from a shipping family and had already been married to an Italian count. She had a snake tattoo and a love of high fashion. The couple married in 1923 and were largely based in London's Grosvenor Square until they moved to Eltham Palace in 1936, sparing no expense on its reinvention.

Through the reigns of Edward II to Charles I, Eltham Palace was a royal household and was, around the time of Henry VIII, even more substantial in scale than Hampton Court. But after the English Civil War (1642–51), the palace was abandoned and fell into slow decline, with the great hall used as a barn during its period as a farmstead. By the time the Courtaulds acquired the site, the fifteenth-century great hall was the only remaining element of the original palace and was converted into a grand music room, forming one wing of the reinvented house.

In 1933, the couple commissioned architects Seely & Paget (John Seely [1899–1963] and

Paul Paget [1901–1985]) to design an opulent new home alongside the great hall, while the flamboyant Italian-born and London-based designer Peter Malacrida (1889–1983) was asked to collaborate on the interiors. The resulting V-shaped building was designed in a 'Wrenaissance' style on the exterior and an exuberant Art Deco on the interior, beginning with the entrance hall. Here, the architects created a dramatic, double-height space topped with a dome punctuated by glass lenses, while a streamlined ribbon window floats over the front door, drawing in light from the porticoed entrance. Swedish designer Rolf Engströmer (1892–1970) was part of the design team,

Opposite Topped by a domed ceiling, the double-height lounge is one of the most theatrical spaces in the house, setting the tone for the rest of the residence from the outset.

Below As befits the most accomplished Art Deco interiors, there is an emphasis on fine craftsmanship, refined materials and exquisite finishes in the dining room.

Below Marquetry, designed by Rolf Engströmer in association with interior designer Peter Malacrida, adds character and drama to the hallway and lounge from which the rest of the house radiates.

Opposite Opulent finishes carry through the circulation spaces and private realm, including the bedrooms and bathrooms. The master bath has a backdrop of golden mosaic tilework and a marble surround.

commissioning the inlaid marquetry wall panelling with pastoral scenes inspired by the couple's time in Italy and two heroic guards either side of the doorway. A lounge under the dome is anchored by a circular rug by celebrated textile designer Marion Dorn (1896–1964).

The exquisite level of Deco detailing and finishing throughout was combined with the use of high technology, ranging from underfloor heating and an integrated vacuum-cleaning system to luxuries such as piped music and an internal telephone system. Two of the most opulent spaces are undoubtedly Malacrida's

oval-shaped master bedroom and adjoining bathroom, where the marble-clad bathtub is set within an arched alcove lined with gold mosaic tiles. Even Virginia's pet lemur, Mah-Jongg, was accommodated in luxury with a bespoke heated cage decorated with jungle scenes.

Briefly, in the late 1930s, Eltham Palace became a focal point for fine society. But in 1945, the Courtaulds moved to Scotland and then Rhodesia, where they built their version of a French château, called La Rochelle. Eltham Palace, now fully restored in its Courtauld-era glory, is cared for by English Heritage.

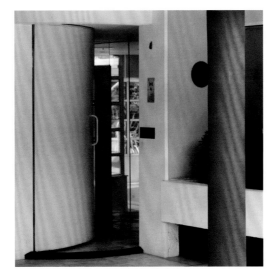

66 FROGNAL
HAMPSTEAD, LONDON
Connell, Ward & Lucas (1938)

The path of Modernist architecture has not always run smoothly in England. There have been periods of reaction when conservatives and traditionalists have fought back, arguing against the forces of change and the 'shock of the new'. Colin Lucas's 66 Frognal, situated on a leafy and picturesque Hampstead street, offers one such case study and became a cause célèbre during the late 1930s with arguments for and against played out in court and within the media.

With New Zealanders Basil Ward (1902–1976) and Amyas Connell (1901–1980), Englishman Colin Lucas (1906–1988) was a partner and principal at Connell, Ward & Lucas, which became known for its innovative and influential Modernist houses in the 1930s, beginning with Connell's High & Over in Buckinghamshire (1931). Lucas designed a pioneering weekend cottage at Bourne End called Noah's House (1929), described as the first monolithic concrete house in the UK, with the partners continuing to author their own individual projects even after joining forces.

Lucas's client for 66 Frognal was solicitor Geoffrey Walford (1902–1968), who wanted to commission a Hampstead home for himself, his wife and their four children. Walford was an eloquent supporter of Modernist architecture and, having found a corner site in Hampstead, asked Lucas to design a substantial, three-storey house suitable for a large family.

To the street, the house was relatively discreet and enclosed. Lucas's design raised the main body of the house on piloti, creating a sheltered undercroft for parking and play, with only the entrance hall and a playroom originally located at ground level. The upper two storeys of the front elevation balance long, thin ribbons of glazing with closed walls of rendered concrete, with a box-like stairwall projecting outwards at the centre. To the rear, however, the house was very different in character, with banks of floor-to-ceiling glass and liner-like decks and terraces that step down towards the private back garden. The main living spaces and master bedroom were at mid-level, with children's bedrooms and a roof terrace on the top floor.

Despite the architect's intention to connect the house to this private realm rather then impose directly upon the streetscape, the

Opposite The house opens itself up to the rear garden, with banks of glass, terraces and decks all connecting with this private enclave.

Above A subtle maritime theme runs through the house, exhibited in the form of its tiered decks, porthole windows, and liner-style walkways and ship's ladders.

Below Recently updated by architect John Allan, 66 Frognal features a sequence of free-flowing family living spaces at mid-level.

Opposite The principal living spaces connect with the adjoining terrace via a floor-to-ceiling wall of glass, while the external stairway links the elevated terrace to the walled garden below.

plans for 66 Frognal were met by neighbours with alarm. One of the most outspoken critics was another architect, Sir Reginald Blomfield (1856–1942), who happened to live on the same street. Blomfield had already clashed, a few years earlier, with Amyas Connell in a BBC radio debate called 'For and Against Modern Architecture', as well as publishing a book, *Modernismus* (1934), attacking Modernist design: 'The new architecture is essentially continental in its origin and inspiration, and claims as a merit that it is cosmopolitan,' said Blomfield. 'I detest and despise cosmopolitanism.'[7]

Lucas's own encounter with Blomfield was more than unfortunate, with the elder architect attacking the plans for 66 Frognal from the start, while another architect turned Conservative politician and member of the London County Council, Sir Robert Tasker (1868–1959), called it 'one of the greatest pieces of vandalism ever perpetuated in London'.[8] After a long delay, the house eventually won planning permission but with conditions on its appearance that Walford objected to, with the solicitor taking his own case to the High Court to win approval for Lucas's intended plans.

Later, in 1938, after the completion of the house, Walford wrote lyrically about his new home for the journal of the Royal Institute of British Architects (RIBA; December 1938).

Above Circulation spaces feature a combination of machine-age references and streamlined elements, as seen in the banister around the staircase.

Opposite The substantial indoor pool at ground-floor level, which overlooks the back garden, was a later addition that made use of the sheltered undercroft and has two floors of living space arranged above it.

'I can only regret that this building should offend the susceptibilities of some people and be beyond the comprehension of others,' Walford concluded. 'To me it has proved to be an experience of intense interest and delight.'[9]

Ultimately, this divisive house received much support from critics, ranging from Nikolaus Pevsner to Ian Nairn. More recently, it has been restored by John Allan of Avanti Architects, taking account of an indoor swimming pool that had been added at ground-floor level and an additional bedroom pavilion on the top floor. Connell, Ward & Lucas broke up in 1939, just one year after 66 Frognal's completion.

  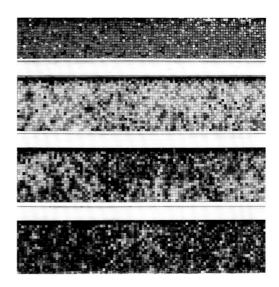

HIGH SUNDERLAND
NEAR SELKIRK, SCOTTISH BORDERS
Peter Womersley (1957)

Opposite The house sits within a rural hillside setting surrounded by mature trees, which provide a sense of tranquillity and a verdant, natural backdrop.

Above Terraces and a car port sit within the rectangular outline of the house and provide halfway points between the interior and exterior; the mosaic wall on the front elevation was designed by Bernat Klein in association with Peter Womersley.

During the mid-1950s, textile designer Bernat Klein (1922–2014) was driving through the Yorkshire countryside with his wife Margaret when he spotted a striking modern house. The couple pulled up, knocked on the door and discovered Farnley Hey, a house designed by architect Peter Womersley (1923–1993) in 1954 as a wedding gift for his brother. Klein contacted the architect soon after and commissioned Womersley to design a new family home, known as High Sunderland, in the Scottish Borders.

Sitting among trees on a gentle plateau accessed via a sloping driveway, the house has been praised as one of the most accomplished buildings designed by Womersley, whose work has only recently won the appreciation it deserves. The story of the house is recorded in a book by Klein's daughter, Shelley Klein, called *The See-Through House* (2020), which documents the collaborative, creative relationship that developed between architect and client:

'We hit it off immediately,' my father recalled almost forty years later. 'We liked his work and then liked Peter. He was shy and quietly spoken yet unostentatiously and firmly self-confident, particularly in relation to his work. Surprisingly to me he was an admirer of Palladio and had a profound knowledge of classical architecture. His professional commitment to the modern house idiom however was total and uncompromising.'[10]

The Kleins had chosen a beautiful setting for their new home, without a neighbour in sight. The parcel of land around High Sunderland extends to just over three acres, with Womersley's linear, single-storey building standing out vividly against the backdrop of mature trees and woodland. Using a steel- and timber-framed structure, the architect created a neat, rectangular outline but one that encompassed not only internal spaces but also an integrated car port and entrance zone, as well as a courtyard and a terrace.

On the outside, architect and client not only made the most of the floor-to-ceiling banks of glass that connect the house to the landscape but they also contrasted wooden

Below The dining area is to one side of the main living space, with an integrated planter acting as a gentle barrier between the two. There is easy access to the adjoining kitchen as well as to a sun terrace alongside.

Right The sunken seating area centres around the fireplace, with its monolithic flue, while additional seating, a study and a library are all arranged around the perimeter of this open-plan space.

cladding with colourful infill panels, including a wall of mosaics around the entry point to the car port and the front door beyond it. Similarly, Womersley and Klein worked closely on the interiors, with travertine floors, timber ceilings and finely crafted joinery complemented by Klein's textiles. The key space in the house is undoubtedly the generous living room, which has a sunken seating area organized around a feature fireplace with additional zones, such as a library wall, a study and a dining area surrounding it. The master suite, meanwhile, was positioned at one end of the house with the children's bedrooms at the other.

Opposite The compact kitchen is separate from the adjoining dining room and fully enclosed, yet benefits from sunlight spilling in from the sun terrace.

Above Like the kitchen, the bathrooms are relatively compact but profit from fitted, space-saving elements; the master bedroom features a storage wall that helps to free up the rest of the space.

A few years after the house was finished, Chanel chose one of Klein's textile designs for part of its Spring 1963 collection. Soon, Klein's work was being taken up by multiple fashion houses – Christian Dior, Yves Saint Laurent and Pierre Cardin – as his reputation and that of his Scottish, mill-made textiles grew internationally. In 1972, Womersley designed a separate and substantial studio a walk away from the house, which was later taken into separate ownership.

Despite damage caused by a chimney fire, High Sunderland has been well looked after. Acquired from the Klein family by new owners, the house has undergone an extensive but sensitive restoration led by Scottish architectural practice Loader Monteith. Services and amenities have been updated, but original features have been retained throughout, with the character of the woodwork and joinery (including maple, rosewood, walnut and idigbo) enhancing the sense of warmth and sitting well with the framed views of the landscape beyond the windows.

Womersley grew frustrated with his work in the UK after a major commission to expand and update the Edinburgh College of Art was scaled back. He spent part of the 1970s and 1980s working in Hong Kong, but also travelled widely. Writing an appreciation in *The Observer* in 2017, critic Rowan Moore described Womersley as 'quite simply, one of the best British architects of the twentieth century, and until recently one of the most overlooked'.[11]

LASLETT HOUSE
CAMBRIDGE, CAMBRIDGESHIRE
Trevor Dannatt (1958)

Opposite The house sits in a garden on a quiet urban street within easy walking distance of a number of Cambridge colleges and the centre of the city.

Above The primary materials are grey Holco cement blocks, brickwork painted white and cedar cladding laid in vertical strips on the upper level.

Sitting quietly on a leafy residential street in Cambridge, the Laslett House is the most accomplished and perhaps the most Nordic of the mid-century houses designed by Trevor Dannatt (1920–2021). The architect first visited Sweden and Denmark in 1947 and was much impressed by the model of Scandinavian Modernism, which offered a tempting source of inspiration during the post-war period, as distinct from the precepts of the International Style and, somewhat later, concrete Brutalism. In its use of natural materials and in its layout, the Laslett House possesses an engaging sense of warmth and welcome.

The house was commissioned by historian Peter Laslett (1915–2001) and his wife, Janet, for themselves and their two sons. Laslett had graduated from Cambridge with a double first and later returned, becoming a fellow at Trinity College and a specialist in demographic history. He published widely and was a co-founder of the Cambridge Group for the History of Population & Social Structure. The Lasletts were introduced to Dannatt by a mutual friend and asked him to design a family home on this garden site, which is within easy walking distance of Trinity College and other central Cambridge colleges.

Dannatt made the most of the garden setting, which offers a degree of privacy and enclosure even within the urban context. The neat, rectangular two-storey building was constructed using grey-painted, cement Holco blocks, plus additional brickwork for the lower level. The upper storey is clad in Western red cedar with the boards fixed vertically. The composition is then topped by a flat roof with a protruding brick chimney.

One of the key decisions was to place the main living room on the upper level of the building, meaning that it benefits from both the garden views and the rich quality of natural light. Timber floors and cedar wall panelling, laid horizontally, give the room an almost treehouse-like quality, while the seating is arranged around the fireplace, where the brickwork surround is painted a crisp, contrasting white. This thoughtful combination of ingredients ensures an inviting Nordic character for the space,

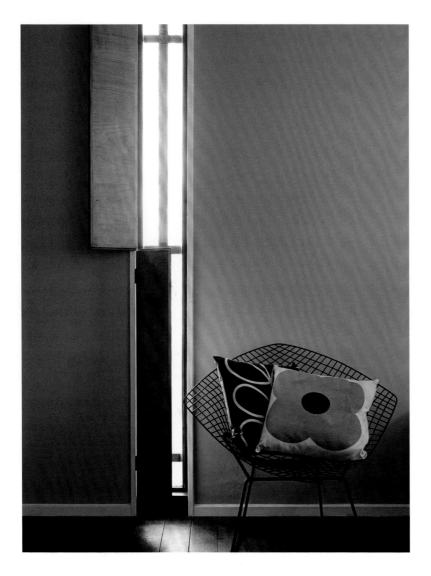

Above Dannatt designed many integrated features throughout, such as the mini shutters over the slot windows. The interiors present a curated choice of mid-century pieces including chairs by Harry Bertoia and Finn Juhl.

Opposite The sitting room is situated on the upper level of the house, overlooking the garden. The cushions on a sofa by Hvidt & Mølgaard form part of the palette of natural colour tones.

which connects at one end with the open stairwell, topped by a modest rectangular skylight. Four family bedrooms are also situated on the upper storey, but are positioned a few steps up from the main living room to create a discreet sense of separation between these two parts of the house.

This layout meant that, apart from the main entrance, the ground floor could largely be devoted to more functional spaces such as the kitchen, a playroom/lounge and an integrated garage/utility room positioned just below the living room. The most engaging space in this part of the house is the dining room, positioned right at the centre of the plan while also connecting with the rear garden through

a triptych of folding doors. The detailing throughout the house was also well conceived and elegantly executed with, for example, integrated timber shutters over the vertical slot windows that can be seen in various parts of the house.

The Grade II-listed building is widely regarded as the finest of Dannatt's houses but is also seen as a key exemplar of the architect's design philosophy. Other listed Dannatt buildings completed over the course of his long professional life include Vaughan College in Leicester (1962) and the Bootham School Assembly Hall in York (1966), as well as earlier projects undertaken with his mentor, Sir Leslie Martin (1908–2000), who invited him to be part

of the team working on the Royal Festival Hall (1951) at the start of his career.

Furthermore, Dannatt pursued a successful parallel life as an architectural writer, curator and critic. His book *Modern Architecture in Britain* was published in 1959, just one year after the completion of the Laslett House. This landmark book featured an entry on the Cambridge house.

Opposite The crafted central stairway doubles as a junction between the sitting room at one end of the upper storey and the family bedrooms at the other, with a gentle shift in floor level between these two zones.

Above The combined kitchen and dining room is on the ground floor and connects with the rear garden and a terrace via a tripartite set of folding glass doors.

LEUCHIE WALLED GARDEN HOUSE
NORTH BERWICK, EAST LOTHIAN
James Dunbar-Nasmith (1960)

Opposite The eighteenth-century walled garden provides a protective enclosure that frames the mid-century house as well as beds and borders full of colour and texture.

Above The run of spaces facing the open garden includes an integrated verandah alongside the sitting room and, at the far end, a gently elevated timber box holding the master bedroom, with an undercroft below leading down to services and storage at basement level.

Offering both a delightful, open aspect and a degree of protective enclosure, the eighteenth-century walled garden at Leuchie presents a picturesque setting for a twentieth-century home. Designed by Edinburgh-based architect James Dunbar-Nasmith (1927–2023), the house provides a fascinating contrast between the old and the 'new', with the latter meaning the mid-century period and the early 1960s in particular.

The house was commissioned by Sir Hew Hamilton-Dalrymple (1926–2018) and his wife, Lady Anne-Louise (1932–2017), as a family home. They were living in nearby Leuchie House, which had been in the family for generations, but decided that it was too big for one family. Wanting to stay within the borders of the family estate, Sir Hew settled on the idea of building a new home in the spacious walled garden, which brought many advantages. Sir Hew was a garden lover and he chose a position that faced south, while an existing gardener's cottage on the boundary wall could, potentially, be amalgamated into the design.

The current Sir Hew Dalrymple and guardian of the Leuchie Walled Garden House explains:

My father was in the army and was then a businessman in Edinburgh. He was a very upright, traditional, conservative man, but he and my mother decided to build this house, which was extraordinary. My brothers and I have never quite worked out how they had the foresight, but I think one reason might have been that James Dunbar-Nasmith was a friend of theirs. He had just qualified as an architect and this was his second private house. What is unique about it is the way that it was designed around the portraits, pictures and furniture that my parents brought from the big house. It's that mix that makes it different to other mid-century houses.

Dunbar-Nasmith was best known as a theatre architect, but there were also residential commissions, including cottages and other buildings on Queen Elizabeth II's Balmoral Estate. Leuchie offered a unique challenge that Dunbar-Nasmith fully embraced, developing a design that made the most of the garden setting while also incorporating

Above Family portraits feature
throughout the interior of the house,
as seen in the entrance hall, where
Sir Hew Dalrymple-Hamilton (1774–1834)
takes centre stage.

Right The generously scaled sitting
room is at the centre of the plan, with
seating facing the fireplace to one side
and open views of the garden to the other;
the Blüthner piano is a family piece.

those elements of family history that were so
important to his clients.

The two-storey gardener's cottage was
reworked and updated, hosting service spaces
such as the kitchen as well as a nursery and
additional bedrooms. For the new building,
Dunbar-Nasmith adopted a linear, one-storey
layout with the house anchored by the garden
wall and cottage to the rear while facing the
open expanse of the central lawn flanked by
elegant borders. Key communal spaces were
placed at the centre of the plan, complemented

Above The new kitchen and adjoining dining area are located in a recently extended part of the house that forms a sequence of open-plan spaces.

Opposite The kitchen and dining zone flow through to the library and lounge, which offers a more casual alternative to the formal sitting room.

by a family dining area to one side plus an integrated verandah. The main run of family bedrooms also looks out onto the walled garden, including the master bedroom suite, which is set within a gently elevated wooden box at the far end of the sequence, floating above the entrance to an undercroft and basement.

While the layout made the most of the views and all available sunlight, the interiors adopted a crafted approach using a palette of warm and largely natural materials. The central hallway and adjoining living room, for example, have muninga parquet floors, spruce ceilings and beech panelling, with a marble fireplace forming a focal point. Family portraits feature throughout, beginning with the full-length portrait of the fourth Sir Hew in the hallway, and add a vibrant layer of historical character.

Reviewing the house in *Country Life* in 1961, under the headline 'Old and New in Harmony', architectural historian Mark Girouard acknowledged: 'The conventional country-house elements of furniture and portraits are all there, but used in a new setting and a new way, so that one has the impression of creative originality instead of a repetition of old formulas.'[12]

A restoration programme by the current Sir Hew and his wife has introduced modern services, heating, insulation and amenities, while respecting the intrinsic personality of the house. A spacious, open-plan family kitchen, dining area and lounge now feature at one end of the house, extending the space into a former side terrace. The walled garden and its borders have also been lovingly revived, with house and grounds once again working in perfect synergy.

SPENCE HOUSE
BEAULIEU, HAMPSHIRE
Basil Spence (1961)

There is a Nordic quality to a number of Basil Spence's most expressive and engaging buildings. For a time, Spence (1907–1976) was described as a 'British Scandinavianist' on account of his appreciation of Nordic Modernism, particularly the way in which architects such as Alvar Aalto (1898–1976) and Arne Jacobsen (1902–1971) responded to context, setting, light and materials. Projects such as Falmer House (1962) and the Meeting House (1967), both at the University of Sussex, have a Nordic sensibility, and the same might also be said of the interiors of the British Embassy in Rome (1971). Yet perhaps the most Scandinavian of Spence's designs is his country retreat, or cabin, alongside the Beaulieu River in Hampshire.

Spence was a keen sailor and found a site with access to the water on the northern bank of the river, in an area to the southeast of the village of Beaulieu described as the point where the New Forest meets the Solent. He carefully positioned the two-storey building on a gentle rise overlooking the river, with mature trees providing a green backdrop and ensuring privacy. The architect created a brick plinth for the timber-framed and cedar-clad building, while cantilevering the timber box holding the piano nobile out over the terrace and adjoining pool at the front of the house. In the original design, the resulting undercroft was largely used for boat storage and a workshop space.

Bedrooms and living spaces were arranged on the upper level. The key area on this floor was always the spacious elevated living room, with its band of picture windows facing the river and its sculptural fireplace in concrete and brick, engineered by Ove Arup. With wooden floors and ceilings, this room especially embraces a Scandinavian-inspired aesthetic full of warmth and welcome.

After using their weekend house for just a few years, London-based Spence and his family decided that they needed more living space. Consequently, the undercroft was converted into a dining room and kitchen, freeing up more sleeping space on the upper level. Spence also added an elegant spiral staircase to one side within a timber and glass cylinder to link the two storeys. The cylinder softens the otherwise

Opposite The orientation of the house makes the most of its hillside position and views over the Beaulieu River, especially from the main living area on the upper level.

Above The house is essentially a timber cabin on a brick plinth; mature trees all around provide privacy and a verdant, natural backdrop.

Above The spiral staircase and its holding drum were added when Spence decided to convert the undercroft into additional living space, thus introducing a new kitchen and dining area at ground-floor level.

Opposite The upstairs living room enjoys the best of the views, while a concrete and brick fireplace to one side offers a focal point for the timber-lined space.

linear building and also hints at Spence's growing interest in circular structures, as seen in the Meeting House at Sussex University and again in the extension to the New Zealand Parliament in Wellington, known as the 'Beehive' (original concept 1964). Spence also designed a separate work studio close by, again using timber, with a monopitch roof over the single-storey structure.

There is an intrinsic modesty to the Beaulieu house, which has recently been fully restored and extended by John Pardey, as well as a sensitive appreciation of the context. Pardey has suggested that, along with the Sussex Meeting House, Spence's Beaulieu home provides 'a

high point in a strand of British architecture that engaged the use of romantic and sculptural forms in an attempt to humanise a modernist language by a fusion with historical precedent'.[13]

Modesty, sensitivity and romance were characteristics that critics found completely lacking in Scottish-born Spence's most controversial project, the Hutchesontown C tower blocks (1962) in the Gorbals district of Glasgow, completed just one year after his own country cabin. Curiously, Spence hoped that his Corbusian twin tower blocks would look like 'a great ship in full sail'[14] when the morning washing fluttered from the balconies on a sunny Scottish day. The reality was very different

Below and opposite The use of natural materials lends the house an almost Scandinavian character, reinforced by Spence's sensitivity to the beauty of the site and setting.

and the blocks were demolished in 1993, as derided almost as much as his greatest project, Coventry Cathedral, also completed in 1962, was praised and applauded.

Accusations of a kind of architectural schizophrenia, with Spence switching from Nordic or Arts and Crafts-inspired contextuality to high Brutalism, did not help with critical assessments of the architect's reputation. Long after he had sold the Beaulieu house, Spence found another country retreat in Suffolk – the sixteenth-century Yaxley Hall – pointing once again to his eclectic tastes. Only in recent years has Spence's work been reviewed and reassessed, resulting in both recognition and listings for many of his buildings.

UPPER LAWN PAVILION
NEAR TISBURY, WILTSHIRE
Alison and Peter Smithson (1962)

Opposite Upper Lawn Pavilion is
perched on the existing stone wall,
running along the boundary of the site,
which is one of a number of historical
remnants incorporated into the design
of the new house.

Above Zinc sheets clad the upper level
of the building, contrasting with both the
timber framework and the banks of glass.

Along with many of their contemporaries, Alison (1928–1993) and Peter (1923–2003) Smithson used their own homes as laboratories for experimentation. With their period London homes, particularly 2 Priory Walk and then Cato Lodge, the Smithsons explored ideas concerning 'found space', seeking to respect the provenance of a given building and the patina of the past while making a very clear distinction between the historical fabric and their own modern interventions. In this way, the architects' family homes were consciously layered.

In their country cottage in Wiltshire, the Smithsons developed these principles further and took them in a fresh direction. During the late 1950s they had bought a derelict farmstead, surrounded by fields and woodland, on the edge of the Fonthill Estate near Tisbury. All that remained of the stone and brick cottage were remnants and relics, apart from one side wall, which also formed part of the enclosure around the old farmyard, and a chimney buttress. These elements were taken as found and incorporated into the design of the new, rectangular building, which was essentially a two-storey,

timber-framed pavilion that used the stone wall and buttress as additional forms of support, as well as providing sources of raw, natural character and texture. A second chimney was removed and the position of the building shifted slightly to create an outdoor room to one side that includes original floor tiles from the cottage and a ghost window in the stone boundary wall that helps partially protect the terrace.

The Smithsons saw Upper Lawn Pavilion, or the Solar Pavilion as it was sometimes called, as a cabin in the countryside rather than a sophisticated retreat. They worked on the house and its surroundings themselves at weekends, developing a tradition of 'camping out' at the pavilion. The space featured banks of sliding teak doors to three elevations on the lower floor as well as extensive glazing in a matching pattern on the upper storey, framed by zinc cladding. This gives the building a rigorous geometry that contrasts vividly with the farmstead setting and the salvaged elements of the old cottage.

Inside, the family embraced the idea of camping out in the design of the interiors,

Opposite The pavilion serves as a belvedere within the landscape, connecting with the walled garden and framing ever-changing views of the shifting seasons.

Above There is a purposeful emphasis upon simplicity and materiality woven into the design of the interior, seen in such elements as the straightforward ship's ladder serving as a staircase.

which were originally quite simple and even rudimentary, with views of the landscape and the changing seasons through the bands of glass always taking centre stage. The lower floor was largely devoted to the kitchen and dining area, adjoining the terrace, and service spaces, while a simple ship's ladder led to the upper floor. Here, the Smithsons used the stone chimney buttress as a partial partition between the main living room at one end and sleeping quarters at the other. Early on, the family simply laid out bedding on the timber floors as needed.

More recently, the house has been fully and carefully restored by architects Sergison Bates, who also sought to respect the idea of found space, preserving original materials where possible. Sergison Bates stripped away inappropriate additions by a previous owner and concentrated on repairing internal damage caused by leakage from rainwater, while also seeking to upgrade the thermal performance of the pavilion by introducing underfloor heating and a new wood-burning stove in the upstairs living room. The extensive glass has been upgraded but is still single glazed.

The Smithsons' weekend retreat proved to be, as with so much of their work, highly influential. This was true of their idea of taking found structure further, incorporating the old into the new, while simultaneously making the difference between past and present

Above and opposite Through its bands of glass, the main living room on the upper storey offers open views over the garden walls, across the surrounding fields and towards the woodland beyond. The wood-burning stoves were upgraded during a recent renovation and restoration process.

explicit. The pavilion also offered, rather like Le Corbusier's simple Cabanon in the south of France (1951), a modern version of an escapist cabin tied to its setting and the landscape.

As with the Cabanon, where Le Corbusier proclaimed himself to be at his happiest, there was a disconnect between the pavilion and the mass Brutalist housing schemes developed by the Smithsons in a Corbusian style, complete with their 'streets in the sky'. Built by a main road and structurally flawed, the couple's controversial Robin Hood Gardens

housing scheme (1972) in London has been criticized as one of the Smithsons' least successful and most alienating projects. It has been partially demolished despite repeated attempts to have the buildings listed and conserved. As with Basil Spence (see p. 97), who designed a Scandinavian-inspired country retreat for himself around the same time as his Gorbals tower blocks, there was a powerful contrast between the Smithsons' ideal of a solar pavilion and their design solution for mass housing.

WIMBLEDON VILLAGE HOUSE
WIMBLEDON, LONDON
Peter Foggo and David Thomas (1963)

Architects Peter Foggo (1930–1993) and David Thomas designed and built a series of highly innovative British houses during the 1960s. They experimented with a range of structural systems and solutions, beginning with the timber-framed Sorrel House near Chichester, completed in 1960, and followed by a number of steel-framed modular homes in Sussex, which took a degree of inspiration from Californian Case Study Houses designed by Craig Ellwood (1922–1992) and others. There were also a handful of houses in south London, including this standalone residence close to the southern edge of Wimbledon Common.

In this suburban setting, Foggo and Thomas designed a mid-century Modern retreat. The single-storey building was built using concrete goal posts that provide a robust structural framework. They are assisted by the side walls at either end of the rectangular building, which are completely closed to neighbouring houses. This approach allowed the architects to create a semi-transparent pavilion with curtains of glass to the front and back, offering a vivid sense of connection to the garden setting.

There is an open-plan living area towards the centre of the pavilion, as well as a service core that held a compact galley kitchen and utility room. A secondary, elevated roofline allowed for the introduction of clerestory windows that bring natural light into the more enclosed parts of the house. Family bedrooms were positioned at each end of the building and later, during the 1970s, an extension was added to one side holding a garage and additional service spaces.

When the house was put up for sale in 2014, it caught the eye of the head of Claremont furnishing fabrics, Adam Sykes, who has a particular love of mid-century Modernism. With architect Matthew Giles, Sykes embarked on a restoration and revival programme that included opening up the main living areas to maximize the sense of space while replacing the inappropriate 1970s extension with a new wing designed in a sympathetic style.

Giles's new addition includes a semi-open-plan kitchen, lounge and dining area, with sliding glass walls connecting the space to the walled garden. The new extension meant that the original galley kitchen and utility room

Opposite The single-storey house is supported by a structural system consisting of a series of concrete goal posts, which also enhance the rhythmic character of the building.

Above The house offers a vivid indoor–outdoor relationship with the recently replanted gardens, which provide a verdant natural backdrop even within this urban setting.

were no longer needed, while the strength and rigour of the structural framework allowed Giles to move partitions and create more spacious and welcoming areas without compromising the character of the building itself. Giles and Sykes collaborated on the interiors, aiming for an aesthetic that felt in keeping with the mid-century style while also introducing contemporary pieces, such as Claremont textiles and twenty-first-century amenities. Sykes says:

I wanted fewer rooms and bigger spaces, along with pocket doors that I loved in the mid-century houses that I saw in Los Angeles. Also none of the clerestory windows were really over rooms that you want to spend much time in, so by

Left The use of a largely external post-and-beam structural framework means that the curtain walls are filled with floor-to-ceiling glass, while the internal layout is highly flexible and adaptable.

Below During the recent renovation programme, the central ceiling coffer was made more visible, with its clerestory windows adding to the rich quality of natural light within the house.

Opposite and below The master
bedroom and bathroom enjoy connections
with the enclosed courtyard garden to the
rear, which provides privacy yet also offers
a tranquil backdrop.

reorganizing the layout we were able to
get light into the most important spaces.
I wanted the house to be really light and
now it has that feeling of an inside-outside
house, where you can literally walk right
through it when the glass doors are open.

The garden was also redesigned, relandscaped
and replanted. The hard surfacing was removed
to create a verdant walled garden, with a path
leading to a porch adapted from the former
car port. 'The original design was interesting,

unusual and so clever…Foggo clearly wanted
to create a very flexible space,' explains Giles.
'We took inspiration from the original design
with our new wing and it creates this L-shaped
plan, which is a really lovely way to live, as you
look across the garden from one part to the other.'

Following on from their pioneering houses
of the 1960s, Foggo and Thomas joined the
architectural unit of Arup Associates, an
appropriate working environment for architects
preoccupied by the relationship between
architecture and structural engineering.

THE AHM HOUSE
HARPENDEN, HERTFORDSHIRE
Jørn Utzon and Povl Ahm (1963)

British-based, Danish-born engineer Povl Ahm (1926–2005) worked with many of the master architects of the mid-century period. This included a collaboration with Arne Jacobsen on St Catherine's College in Oxford and such key projects with Basil Spence as Coventry Cathedral and the University of Sussex (see p. 97). Ahm was also an influential part of the team at Ove Arup & Partners who were trying to work out, during the late 1950s and early 1960s, exactly how to build Jørn Utzon's majestic but highly complex Sydney Opera House with its dynamic roofline of intersecting concrete sails. Around the same time Ahm asked Utzon (1918–2008) if he could design a house for him in Harpenden.

From the early 1950s, Ahm was based in Arup's London office. '[He] intended to be here for two years and then go back to Denmark,' said Ahm's wife, Birgit, in 2008. 'We had known each other since schooldays in Aarhus. We got married six months after he started over here and he loved it, so we stayed.'[15]

With a growing family to think about, Ahm secured a parcel of land on a quiet suburban street in Harpenden. He sent Utzon site drawings and photographs, and asked whether the architect would produce a design for him. Although he was never able to visit in person, Utzon obliged and sent Ahm a set of plans that the engineer began to turn into reality.

Utzon's design owed more to his own family home in Denmark and other early residential projects than to the Opera House. It is essentially an elegant pavilion stretching back lengthways on the site to overlook the rear garden. Given that the street alongside is at a lower level than the garden, a car port was created next to the road itself while also sheltering the front door; steps then lead up into the pavilion.

Family bedrooms, bathrooms and a compact kitchen were arranged at one end of this principal level but the key space is the generous living area: an inviting, open room with walls of glass overlooking the adjoining terraces and the garden. It is a beautifully crafted space, with a roof supported by a combination of monumental concrete trusses and 20m-long beams, fully exposed and expressed. These contrast with the boundary wall and fire

Opposite The main living spaces are located in a single-storey pavilion that stretches out into the rear garden.

Above The pavilion provides a vivid indoor–outdoor relationship, with walls of floor-to-ceiling glass connecting the family living area to the adjoining terraces and the garden beyond.

surround made of Aylesbury buff brick and pale Höganäs Swedish tiles for the floor, of a similar kind to those used to coat the sculpted roof canopies of the Opera House. The main seating area is arranged around the fireplace, while a secondary lounge is lightly distinguished by its position one step up, at the same level as the terrace beyond the banks of glass. This combination of colours and textures, including the timber ceiling strips between the concrete beams, creates a space full of warmth and light, while the inside–outside relationship is vivid and engaging.

Recent restoration work by architects Coppin Dockray, commissioned by the current

Left A gentle shift in floor level within the garden pavilion allows for two distinct seating zones in one open-plan living space; furniture by Arne Jacobsen within the upper zone adds to the mid-century Scandinavian-inspired aesthetic.

Below Towards the other end of the pavilion, the fireplace with its brick surround draws the sofa and seating to it; the dining area and kitchen can be glimpsed along the hallway.

Opposite The combination of Aylesbury buff brickwork and bespoke joinery creates a warm palette of tones and textures that carries through both the circulation spaces and the key rooms, such as the kitchen.

Above The master bedroom sits within the newer section of the house, added by Povl Ahm during the 1970s; the Vitra-produced chaise by the window is a design by Charles and Ray Eames.

owners, has helped to revitalize the living space and the dining area alongside it, which has a serving hatch through to the galley-style kitchen. The original bedrooms in this part of the house feature fitted wardrobes and shelving set into the brickwork, while the long circulation corridor also holds integrated elements such as desks and dressing tables.

During the early 1970s, Ahm decided that the family needed more living space, so he added a single-storey wing set at right angles to the master building and the car port. This addition sits on the lower portion of the site, turning its back to the street, and offers space for a much larger master suite and more family rooms. Later still, a subterranean link was introduced to tie the two wings together without passing through the covered car port. Each of these

subservient additions – and subsequent updates – has taken into account the original palette of materials chosen by Utzon and Ahm, as well as the need to respect the character of the first and most significant part of the house.

Sympathetically furnished and fully restored, the Ahm House can be seen as a mid-century exemplar of the Danish style set down in suburban Hertfordshire. Certainly, as seen from the perspective of the escapist living room and the secluded back garden, it is possible to completely forget where you are and embrace the Nordic character of this exceptional home, which is the only Jørn Utzon building in the UK.

TURN END

HADDENHAM, BUCKINGHAMSHIRE
Peter Aldington (1965)

Opposite The home sits within gardens lovingly revived and replanted by the Aldingtons and their team, providing a walled oasis within the village.

Above The architecture of the three neighbouring houses and the surrounding gardens form part of one organic, unified plan with constant synergy between interior and exterior space.

While the architecture of Peter Aldington's Turn End and its two neighbouring houses is of undoubted importance, it is its relationship with the surrounding gardens that forms one of the most engaging aspects of this inventive project. In the Buckinghamshire village of Haddenham, Aldington (b. 1933) and his wife Margaret found a site to create a new home that sat alongside an overgrown garden, which once belonged to the Victorian house nearby. The restored, revived and extended garden has become just as important as the three houses themselves.

'With the garden, the ethos was – and still is – to maintain as much of your assets as possible,' says Aldington. 'Part of the garden was the orchard of the Victorian house and it hadn't been touched for sixteen years, we were told. But we only took down one old pear tree, which produced pears that were useful as cobbles. The trees are still our assets.'

Over time, the Aldingtons were able to acquire other small slivers and parcels of land to take the gardens close to an acre, offering a mesmerizing journey from one courtyard or walled garden to another around Turn End and

its neighbours. Although the Aldingtons did not draw an official master plan of the garden, its organic evolution and planting became an intrinsic part of the Haddenham project.

Aldington had considered becoming a gardener, or landscape designer. But architect George Grenfell-Baines (1908–2003), a family friend, suggested that he pursue architecture first and then, if he wished, specialize in landscape design. Aldington took his advice, studying at the University of Manchester and then taking a post with London County Council's architecture department. Having met Margaret, he began to think about building a home. He was drawn to Buckinghamshire after designing his first house there, called Askett Green (1963), on the edge of Princes Risborough.

'We wanted to build a house and felt it was more responsible to build something on a little bit of village,' says Aldington, who was thinking about funding the project by also developing adjoining houses for sale. 'So we started looking for plots with a limit of six houses. We didn't know anything about Haddenham, but we thought it was a village

Opposite The living room is a double-height space, with the master bedroom to one side; a mezzanine level is accessible by ladder.

Below The kitchen and dining area, as well as the master bedroom, connect with a private and courtyard garden that features a water pool and planting suited to the sheltered setting.

with a very distinctive character because of its "wychert" mud walls.'

The Aldingtons secured a site at auction and found a bank manager who agreed to lend them enough to start work on their own house, on the understanding that the other two houses – The Turn and Middle Turn – would be sold on to fund the project. Aldington gave up his job and the couple began work on the new development, project managing the entire process and working closely with local builders and artisans.

Just as the gardens evolved in an organic way, so did the three houses. The interlinked buildings benefit from both communal space and private courtyards, while sharing a similar design language and palette of materials that were established initially in Turn End. Walls made of wychert, or cob, contrast with walls made of cement blocks, while timber is used extensively, along with 30-cm clay floor tiles.

The plan of the house revolves around the surrounding gardens and secluded courtyard with its own water pool. There are various shifts in height, floor level and volume throughout, such as a spacious double-height living room on one side of the spinal hallway and the master

Opposite The double-height living area features integrated, wrap-around seating facing the fireplace, with sunlight pouring in through the clerestory windows above.

Above The master bedroom sits across the spinal hallway from the living area, with connections to both a micro garden at one end and the enclosed courtyard; additional bedrooms are arranged in an adjoining wing a few steps up from the kitchen.

suite on the other, topped by a mezzanine sleeping platform. The gardens seem to spill into the master bedroom itself, with a collection of pot plants against a textural cob wall to one side and the bed facing the garden court to another.

The kitchen and dining area are at the heart of the layout, also looking onto the private court, while Peter's study sits alongside the doorway to the shared parking lot; further bedrooms and the family bathroom sit a few steps up from the kitchen. Initial work was completed in 1965, with the Aldingtons then building the two other houses, before finally circling back to finish Turn End. Aldington soon found commissions in the area, working initially from home and then in a dedicated office, where he was joined by partner John Craig and, eventually, Paul Collinge.

Turn End has remained the Aldingtons' home ever since and is now listed, along with the two neighbouring houses, while the gardens have continued to flourish. In 1998, the Turn End Trust was formed to secure the future of the setting and enable occasional public access to the gardens. 'All I really wanted to do here was not build detached houses,' explains Aldington, who developed his ideas for English courtyard living around the same time that architects such as Jørn Utzon (see p. 115) were following similar approaches in Scandinavia. 'I wanted to build something that could demonstrate how you could build three houses, or thirty houses, according to the amount of land. That was the idea, with one of the three for ourselves.'

CREEK VEAN
FEOCK, CORNWALL
Team 4 (1966)

Opposite The house is divided into
two distinct parts, with a semi-
subterranean link between them
positioned under the outdoor stairway,
which runs down the hillside.

Above The hillside site enjoys open
views over the creek, while the mature
evergreen trees around the house
offer a green backdrop all year round.

Overlooking a picture-postcard Cornish estuary, Creek Vean is one of the most significant houses within the evolution of late-twentieth-century British Modernism in general and High Tech in particular. The house represents the early union of the most influential English architects to emerge during the 1960s and 1970s, offering the members of Team 4 an opportunity to launch their practice and explore seminal ideas that fed into later work. Creek Vean is also a delightful and extraordinary home, which connects with its hillside setting and an engaging vista.

Team 4 was formed in 1963 by architects Norman (b. 1935) and Wendy Foster (née Cheesman, 1937–1989) with Richard (1933–2021) and Su Rogers (né Brumwell, b. 1939), who had met as students at Yale University. Creek Vean was their first project after graduation, commissioned by Su's parents, Marcus and Irene Brumwell, who had bought a bungalow on a sloping site in Feock, looking down on the tidal waters of the creek. Team 4 persuaded them to take on the design of a new and original house.

Marcus Brumwell (1901–1983) was a highly influential figure in the world of post-war design. He was a co-founder, along with Misha Black (1910–1977) and Milner Gray (1899–1997), of the Design Research Unit, which was one of the first multidisciplinary English studios, eventually combining advertising, graphics, industrial design and architecture under one roof. The Brumwells were also art lovers, with a significant collection of work by post-war British artists, and also a piece by Piet Mondrian, which was sold to help pay for Creek Vean.

The house responds to the view down to the creek but also to the sloping topography, with entry via a bridge from the narrow roadway behind the building. Team 4 decided to divide the house into two interconnected parts, which step down the hillside with a ziggurat-style sequence of stairs between them that spills down to the garden below. This arrangement not only allows for the framing of key sight lines, but also offers a neat distinction between the more communal spaces and the family bedrooms.

The main living areas sit within a two-storey wing. They include the main entrance on the upper level and a mezzanine-style living space that faces the view but also looks down onto

Below The combined kitchen and dining area is situated on the lower floor of the two-level wing, with the sinuous, kidney-shaped island one of the many original features in the sensitively restored house.

Right The sitting room is on the upper level of the house, which enjoys an open panorama of the creek; the narrow stairway to one side leads up to the roof.

a central void, or atrium, on the floor below. Stepping down, the lower storey holds a sizeable open-plan kitchen and dining room, which also benefits from the extensive wall of glass looking towards the water. A discreet route under the ziggurat stairway and bridge connects with the second, single-level wing of the house, where a spinal corridor towards the rear of the plan provides access to a studio and bedrooms.

'The building attempts to fit more snugly into its waterfront surroundings by generating a garden on the roof,' Norman Foster once said of the house, which features planting on top of the bedroom wing. 'As this starts to become overgrown, the house will recede into its creek-side Cornish setting.'[16]

For the house itself, which was listed by English Heritage/Historic England in 1998, Team 4 used Forticrete concrete blocks and blue-slate floors. The solidity of these materials contrasts with the banks of glass, which were originally held in place by neoprene gaskets. This detailing, along with bespoke fitted elements such as the sinuous kitchen island, was suggestive of the High Tech path followed, in different ways, by both Foster and Rogers after the dissolution just a few years later in 1967 of Team 4, and the establishment of two of the most successful practices in British architectural history.

The Brumwell family decided to build a second home nearby, known as Pillwood House (1974). Also designed by the Brumwells' daughter, in association with John Miller (b. 1930), who Su married after her divorce from Richard Rogers, Pillwood was listed in 2017.

Following the sale of Creek Vean, it was subsequently bought by architect Richard Dickinson and his wife, Gill. The Dickinsons have lovingly but lightly restored the house, keeping original features such as the kitchen island, while also reviving the garden.

'We absolutely love it and even after many years we still see different angles and different views, as well as things that we hadn't noticed before,' says Richard. 'It's very inspirational and you do spot repeating elements that appear in the later work. But how much at Creek Vean is Foster and how much is Rogers is still an interesting question.'

DR ROGERS HOUSE
WIMBLEDON, LONDON
Richard Rogers (1969)

Opposite The structural steelwork of the house is not only explicitly expressed but accentuated through the use of colour, with vivid yellows for the framework and other elements, such as the kitchen units.

Above The design of the main house and a secondary pavilion makes the most of the garden setting, with a vivid sense of connection to the surroundings even in its suburban context.

'It was very much a prototype,' said Richard Rogers (1933–2021) of the 1960s house he built for his parents in south London, which he always regarded as a key project in the evolution of his work. 'You can make a direct link from the Wimbledon house to the Pompidou Centre. It's all there – the exposed steel frame, the bright colours, as well as flexibility and adaptability.'[17]

The project was finished just two years before Rogers won the career-changing competition to design the Pompidou Centre, in conjunction with Renzo Piano (b. 1937), a project that took from 1971 to 1977. It came three years after completing Creek Vean in collaboration with his colleagues at Team 4, namely Norman and Wendy Foster and his then wife, Su Rogers, whose parents were their clients (see p. 127).

The Wimbledon house was another familial commission, but one that took Rogers in a fresh direction. Dr Nino and Dada Rogers and their children had emigrated from Italy in 1939 and eventually settled in the suburbs of Surrey. As they began thinking about their retirement years, they decided to commission a new house in Wimbledon that would be on a single level and within easy walking distance of both Wimbledon Common and the village. There would be a small home consulting room for Rogers's father and a pottery studio for his mother, and they wanted a certain degree of flexibility threaded throughout the layout.

Around that time, Rogers was already thinking about steel-framed buildings that could, potentially, be mass produced to meet the growing need for new housing. He also drew inspiration from the Californian Case Study Houses designed during the post-war period by Craig Ellwood, Charles and Ray Eames and others, many of which Rogers had visited after completing his studies at Yale University.

'We wanted to use an open-ended steel framework made up of elements that could be bought over the counter, shall we say, with standard steel joints and prefabricated panels,' explained Rogers. 'It had to have very high insulation levels, as we were conscious of the energy crisis, but we managed to build the house from components which were ready made.'

Using this construction system, Rogers designed two complementary pavilions for the

suburban site. He placed the smaller pavilion, holding the pottery studio and a guest bedroom, towards the front of the site and close to the nearby road. Along with the surrounding gardens, which were another priority for Rogers's parents, the studio serves as a buffer between the arterial roadway and the main residence. One of the most striking elements is the sense of transparency, with the exposed steel frame – picked out in bright yellow paintwork – enabling glass curtain walls to the front and back, while the two sides of the house, facing the neighbouring residences, are largely enclosed.

Inside, the structural framework allowed the kind of fluidity and malleability required. Half of the house was left largely open plan, with space

Left A substantial part of the master pavilion is devoted to an open-plan living area, with zones for seating and eating, as well as a run of kitchen units and counters to one side.

Below The transparency of the house, with light flowing through from front to back, enriches the interiors while the integrated yellow blinds match the painted steelwork.

Below The flexibility of the floor plan allows for various permutations in terms of zoning and the arrangement of furniture, with bedrooms and bathroom running in a line beyond the pea-green partition walls.

Opposite During the period that Ab Rogers and his young family lived in the house, the designer embraced the bold use of colour in his own furniture designs and installations, including bunk beds for his children and other bespoke pieces.

enough for the kitchen and dining and sitting areas. A simple set of partition walls divided off the more private spaces in the other half of the house, holding the bedrooms and bathroom, as well as the study and consulting room.

The adaptability of the house has been proven on many occasions. After the death of Nino and Dada Rogers, it became home to their grandson, designer Ab Rogers, and his young family. More recently, the house – also known as Parkside – was gifted to Harvard Graduate School of Design, and was sensitively restored by architect Philip Gumuchdjian (b. 1958).

Back in the late 1960s and 1970s, Richard Rogers himself was delighted at the way in which his parents embraced and enjoyed their home and garden. It remained one of his favourite projects, exhibiting so many of the trademark touches, including the use of colour, that carried through to the architect's later work.

'I always compare my buildings to children and you can't have a favourite child,' Rogers said. 'But the buildings that I have enjoyed most are my parents' house, because it had these embryonic ideas that have influenced us ever since, the Pompidou Centre, because of the fantastic opportunity in Paris to create this people's palace with Renzo Piano, and then the Lloyd's Building and Madrid's Barajas Airport. There is a very direct link between all of them.'

ADILA
NEAR NOTTINGHAM, NOTTINGHAMSHIRE
David Shelley (1970)

Opposite The house has been carefully pushed into the sloping site, with the ground floor providing an entrance sequence and ancillary spaces, with the main living areas and bedrooms above.

Above The house offers constant connections with the natural surroundings, and the extensive use of stone and timber gives Adila an organic, contextual quality.

Surrounded by mature oak trees and Scotch pines, Adila makes the most of its enticing woodland setting. The house is one of just a dozen or so homes built in the woods here, not far from Newstead Abbey and to the north of Nottingham, during the 1960s and 1970s. Designed by architect David Shelley (1934–2012), who worked on a number of mid-century houses in Nottinghamshire and Derbyshire, this house sits within a 2-acre site and has been gently tucked into the sloping topography.

Buttress walls of stonework anchor Adila to its surroundings, but the majority of the house is constructed from steel and glass, with inspiration drawn from the legendary post-war Case Study programme in California, which saw *Arts & Architecture* magazine promoting exemplary houses by architects such as Craig Ellwood (1922–1992), Pierre Koenig (1925–2004) and John Lautner (1911–1994). Banks of floor-to-ceiling glass ensure a constant connection to the landscape and protected green spaces around the residence.

Adila was originally the home of the Coward family, with the name itself said to be a variation on the name of Coward's Nottinghamshire company, Alida Packaging. Having bought the site and commissioned David Shelley, the businessman spared no expense on the house, investing in characterful hardwoods and crafted finishes throughout, including rosewood wall panelling, teak ceilings and terrazzo floors. An indoor swimming pool also formed part of the brief, along with a fish pond.

Shelley decided to push the house into a gentle bank on the site, while preserving the existing trees around it. This created the opportunity for a partial lower level that holds the main entrance and hallway, an integrated car port, additional service spaces and a home office. From the timber-panelled hallway, a spiral staircase leads up to the piano nobile, which stretches back into the grounds in a broadly U-shaped formation.

The layout of the principal living spaces is fluid and informal, with connections to the outdoors maximized wherever possible. Many of these key areas circulate around an internal courtyard garden, which draws in

Below The use of stonework helps to tie the house to the site yet also provides texture and character, especially in combination with the timber ceilings.

Right The sunken conversation pit offers a room within a room; it is an intimate den with seating facing the fireplace and the option to draw a wrap-around curtain on a ceiling-mounted track for greater intimacy.

additional natural light through its walls of floor-to-ceiling glass as well as providing glimpses of the sky above.

One of the most engaging spaces is the sunken conversation pit with wrap-around seating facing a fireplace but also offering views through the courtyard to the kitchen. Ceiling-mounted tracked curtains can be drawn around the conversation pit to enclose it during the evenings and create a more intimate setting, while the natural textures of the joinery and other materials add to the sense of character.

The principal living room sits alongside the conversation pit, lightly distinguished by a subtle change in floor level and a shift in material from terrazzo flooring around the sunken section to timber. Here, again,

Opposite The orientation and positioning of the house mean that the family bedrooms enjoy both privacy and links with the rear gardens.

Above The house is intelligently integrated with outdoor spaces, such as the terraces, courtyards and garden. More indulgent elements such as the pool enjoy framed connections with the outdoors.

the combination of wooden panelling, teak ceilings and granite for a buttress wall projecting outwards to the exterior lends the interiors an organic quality. A bedroom wing and pool house to the rear help to frame the adjoining terraces, with the vivid indoor–outdoor relationship maintained throughout.

The house is now owned by Simon and Monica Siegel, who are co-founders and directors of Atomic in Nottingham, which specializes in twentieth- and twenty-first-century furniture and lighting. The couple, who have carefully restored and updated the house, are dedicated admirers of the Case Study style and have embraced Adila and the setting, which is accessed by a single track running through the woods. Simon Siegel says:

We were immediately struck by the layout and the materials used. The architecture makes the most of the woodland setting and the views out to the trees at the front, as well as the water pool and garden to the rear. But the most commented-upon aspect is that it really feels like a comfortable, liveable home even though it is primarily an open-plan, glass-walled house. We think that's probably down to the materials, like the rosewood and teak, and the house does have a very warm feeling.

CAPEL MANOR HOUSE

HORSMONDEN, KENT
Michael Manser (1971)

British Modernist architect Michael Manser (1929–2016) is best known for a series of innovative steel-framed houses designed and built during the 1960s and early 1970s. Such buildings owe much to the example of Ludwig Mies van der Rohe (1886–1969) and the pioneering Californian Case Study programme of the mid-century period, yet Manser successfully fused such points of inspiration with a contextual response to decidedly British settings and situations. Chief among his projects is Capel Manor House in Kent.

The building was commissioned by the MP John Howard (1913–1982) and his wife Maisie, both of whom became good friends with the architect. The brief, as summed up by John Partridge in *The Architectural Review*, was 'to provide a spacious, easily maintained, single-storey weekend retreat for use later as a retirement home'.[18] Conversations about the house began before the Horsmonden site had even been found, yet the extraordinary surroundings eventually became a key factor of the project.

The 2½-acre site that the Howards settled on, sitting on the edge of the village, was once occupied by a nineteenth-century Gothic mansion designed by Thomas Henry Wyatt (1807–1880) for textile baron Frederick Austen. The house had already been demolished, but the gardens remained, including an elevated terrace with steps down to a sunken garden bordered by an elegant loggia. This inviting plateau, looking out onto the grounds and mature trees, offered a golden opportunity that Manser – and his clients – embraced wholeheartedly.

The new building is essentially a glass-walled pavilion, on a relatively modest scale, that connects with its surroundings in the most intimate, vivid and constant way. At the centre of the plan is a welcoming living room with a sunken seating area arranged around the fireplace. At one end of the house sits the kitchen, while two bedrooms are at the other end, complemented by two compact bathrooms within an adjoining service core. An existing basement, left over from the Victorian building, was repurposed for services and storage.

Below Partition walls around a small study were removed to create a more spacious kitchen and dining area during recent renovations, enhancing the sense of open space and connections to the gardens.

Right The sunken living area is at the centre of the house, with seating arranged around the fireplace. Walls of glass frame the surrounding trees and open views across the gardens.

Internally, Manser specified 'dark-blue brindled' floor tiles, brickwork for the internal walls and timber-strip ceilings, yet importantly the steel framework was fully and openly expressed. A rectangular colonnade alongside the house, which was all that remained of a winter garden, was retained to lightly define and protect a swimming pool. 'What sets this house apart from others of the same pattern is its setting and the use the architects have made of everything that this exceptional site offers,' said Partridge in his report for *The Architectural Review*.[19]

The Howards enjoyed the house for many years, often inviting Manser and his family to spend time with them in Kent. It is now home to television-producer-turned-life-coach Remy Blumenfeld and his partner, artist Henryk Hetflaisz. Blumenfeld has gently restored and updated Capel Manor House, while also commissioning architect Ewan Cameron to design a sympathetic guest lodge nearby. Two years after the restoration was completed, in 2011, the house was listed by English Heritage/Historic England, with praise for the 'absolute refinement of plan and form, executed with precision and a high quality of detail'.[20]

'Michael Manser was delighted by the listing as none of his other houses had been listed at that point,' comments Blumenfeld. 'Perhaps it was because it was designed for friends of his and that he enjoyed spending some time here and because of the site. When he came to visit he was also delighted that everything looked more or less the same as it had when he built it. I definitely got the sense that Capel Manor House was his favourite.'

HOPKINS HOUSE
HAMPSTEAD, LONDON
Michael and Patty Hopkins (1976)

The British High Tech movement that began
in the 1960s and early 1970s was founded on
the idea of making the most of new technologies
and structural engineering to create lighter, more
efficient and more adaptable buildings. This was
the start of the majestic super shed and modular
building systems that could accommodate a
wide range of uses within and, potentially,
grow at will. Materials and structural systems
were boldly expressed through steelwork, and
beams and struts were often picked out in bright
colours, along with services, lifts and ducts.
Banks of glass were also used to the full, creating
semi-transparent structures that added to a
futuristic sense of architectural lightness.

Among the key pioneers of High Tech
architecture in the UK were Richard Rogers
(see pp. 127 and 133), Norman Foster (see p. 127)
and Michael (b. 1935) and Patty (b. 1942) Hopkins.
Having initially worked in partnership with
Foster, Michael Hopkins established Michael
Hopkins & Partners with his wife in 1976. Their
house in Hampstead provided not only a way of
testing out their ideas but also a base for their
practice, as well as serving as the family home.

The couple and their three young children
had previously lived in nearby Highgate, but
needed more living space. They came across
a garden site in Hampstead that had once
belonged to the house next door, with planning
permission already agreed to replace a garage
and studio with a new pair of brick houses.
The Hopkins only wanted to build a single house
but also needed to carefully manage their limited
budget, having invested most of the money from
their previous house in buying the site.

'We decided that we wanted to build a steel-
framed house,' says Patty Hopkins. 'We wanted
to expose the frame and create a grid but we
also wanted it to flow, so we only designed a
few solid partitions. We already had an old
timber-framed house in Suffolk and, although
it was completely different to this house, we
enjoyed the element of an exposed frame.
This was like doing a modern equivalent.'

As with Richard Rogers and the seminal
house he built for his parents in Wimbledon
(see p. 133), the Hopkinses were influenced by
innovative post-war American steel-framed
houses, such as the Eames House in California

Opposite The two-storey home is a
discreet presence in the streetscape, sitting
quietly in its garden setting and at a lower
height than neighbouring buildings.

Above A bridge provides the entry point
from the adjoining street to the upper level
of the steel-framed house, where a spiral
staircase ties the two floors together.

Below The design of the steel framework ensures that the internal spaces remain flexible, with screens, partitions and furniture installations used to define various zones within the home.

Opposite Structural steelwork and key elements such as the prefabricated staircase are picked out in vivid blue paintwork.

(1949) and Mies van der Rohe's Farnsworth House in Plano, Illinois (1951). All of these ideas and influences neatly coalesced in the disciplined design of their new home, which adopts the key characteristics of the High Tech movement, being lightweight, semi-transparent and adaptable.

The house is also very discreet. Given the sloping topography of Hampstead, the garden site is set down from the level of the adjoining street, meaning that the lower storey of the two-storey building almost disappears and a slim steel drawbridge connects the front gate to the front door, which is located on the upper storey.

While making the most of the opportunity to build for themselves, the couple took a pragmatic attitude to the budget and programme. They invested around £20,000 in the steel frame and enclosing the building, while introducing services and the central spiral staircase that connects the two storeys. Initially, however, they made do with very few partition walls, simply using blinds to divide the family bedrooms and living spaces at lower-ground level. This level offers a vivid sense of connection to the private rear garden via banks of floor-to-ceiling glass set within the cross-braced steel framework.

Opposite The upper storey of the house was once used as offices for the Hopkinses' architectural practice but was later reclaimed as family living space.

Above Bedrooms and more private spaces are lightly divided from communal family zones in a highly adaptable layout.

Originally, the Hopkinses' new practice was based upstairs, which benefited from direct access to the street.

The couple managed the building process themselves, from the pad foundations for the steel frame to the aluminium siding on the end walls and the installation of the glazing. Elements such as the staircase and shower room were prefabricated and arrived in one piece, ready for installation.

Later, the architects installed partitions to lend greater privacy to the bedrooms, and eventually the expanding practice moved to dedicated offices. This allowed the family to colonize the upper storey and successfully expand their own living space. Patty Hopkins explains:

The flexibility of it was very successful. It has been used for very different things – an office, a home for a family with children, and now it's just the two of us most of the time. And it was certainly a showcase for the practice to begin with and clients came here to see the house. It seemed right to be living and working out of this space and many of our early buildings were also steel framed.

THE COSMIC HOUSE
HOLLAND PARK, LONDON
Charles Jencks and Terry Farrell (1983)

Charles Jencks (1939–2019) wrote of his own family home, The Cosmic House:

> Symbolic architecture fulfils a desire. Of that I can be sure for a simple reason. When I show sceptics around this house… they inevitably start 'reading' the building in ways I have not intended, finding plausible new connections, extending the plot in unforeseen ways. Once they begin to understand the architecture has meanings, they expect to find more, and thereby discover new ones. The search for meaning in architecture, apparently, is as natural and desired as it is in life.[21]

Jencks's home in Holland Park, originally known as The Thematic House, is certainly a unique text that conveys its author's thoughts about architecture, design, the cosmos and our place in the universe. From the front door to the rear garden, the house is full of symbols, references and footnotes that offer a Postmodern manifesto made real. As such, the house can be seen as a kind of adjunct to his landmark book, *The Language of Post-Modern Architecture* (1977), which Jencks was working on at around the same time as the house.

Charles and Maggie Jencks began working on the family home in 1978, with the ambition of completely reinventing their early Victorian house, dating from the 1840s. Working in close collaboration with architect Terry Farrell, Jencks effectively rebuilt the house behind the period façade, reworking the interiors and the layout of the building, including the spiralling Solar Stair topped by a skylight and a secondary aperture to the sky known as the Moonwell. The rear of the house was transformed to create an abstract face overlooking the back garden, which was designed by Maggie Jencks.

Thematic symbolism carries through the entire house and appears within every room. Jencks broke these themes down into seventeen categories, beginning with a handful of inter-related cosmic topics (which led him to ultimately rename the house) followed by a series of architectural and historical concepts and, lastly, a set of more personal subjects largely expressed in emblems and motifs,

Opposite The rear elevation – or 'face façade' – was extensively reworked by Charles Jencks and Terry Farrell, establishing vivid connections with the garden.

Above Cosmology and references to the solar system are threaded through the interior of the house, while the Time Garden to the rear was designed by Maggie Jencks, including the Future Pavilion – a mirrored door to nowhere inscribed with the words 'the future is behind you'.

Below The Winter Room features a fireplace designed by Michael Graves; the bust of Hephaestus, Greek god of fire, is by Celia Scott (b. 1947).

Opposite The bay window in the Summer Room, which overlooks the back garden, is occupied by a bespoke Sun Table and Chairs; the kitchen alongside is designed around the theme of an Indian summer.

but also recognizing the contributions of family and friends, including designers and architects such as Michael Graves (1934–2015) and Piers Gough (b. 1946), as well as Farrell.

'Instead of proclaiming certainties of belief, it uses hypotheses of science and conventional wisdom as guidepoints,' explained Jencks of his home. 'The notion is that in a secular age there are still objective standards, worthy of symbolic expression by architecture, art and ornament, and these are standards by which we orient ourselves.'[22]

The ground-floor living spaces are based on the five seasons, including – as Jencks said

– an Indian summer. They all revolve around the Solar Stair, which features fifty-two sculpted concrete treads. The focal point in the Winter Room, the primary sitting room, is a fireplace designed by Michael Graves, while the Summer Room is devoted to dining and overlooks the rear garden. Every room and every surface carries a narrative of its own, with these stories often playful in character. Materials are seldom precious and include the multiple use of painted MDF. Illusions fused with architectural twists and turns are a common thread, yet the ideas and intent behind these spaces remain serious and erudite throughout.

Opposite and above left The Solar Stair sits at the heart of the house and was designed by Jencks and Farrell in consultation with astronomer Derek McNally. It features fifty-two steps to represent the weeks of a solar year; each step is marked with an astrological sign devised by Jencks.

Above right The Architectural Library was designed by Jencks as a 'city of books', featuring a series of bookcases and 'slide scrapers' made using repurposed and repainted prefabricated office furniture.

Other key rooms are the upstairs library and study, forming the literal heart of a house where Jencks both lived and worked, with his career encompassing writing, criticism, architecture, interior design and landscape design. Another dynamic space is the master bedroom, which Jencks recognized had a touch of Charles Rennie Mackintosh (see p. 27) in its aesthetic, yet – as with every other room in the house – it is ultimately more complex, nuanced and layered. Gough worked with Jencks on the design of the jacuzzi, which was enjoyed more for its own unique narrative than its functionality, with the water usually so cold that it was seldom used.

In the later years of his life, Jencks decided that the house should be opened to the public after his death, and he collaborated with his daughter, architect Lily Jencks (see p. 267), on the design of a dedicated museum at lower-ground-floor level. The Jencks Foundation was established to care for the Grade I-listed residence, which might be compared to the Pennsylvania home of fellow Postmodern pioneers Robert Venturi (1925–2018) and Denise Scott Brown (b. 1931), also richly layered with symbolism, motifs and meanings.

'The house was a complex collaboration with many different people, including my mother Maggie,' recalls Lily Jencks. 'And that was one of the key ideas of Postmodernism – that it is polyphonic, that it speaks with lots of voices.'

Above The design of the master bedroom, or Foursquare Room, hints at a debt to Charles Rennie Mackintosh, but Jencks also referenced Palladio, Robert Adam, John Soane and Frank Lloyd Wright.

Opposite The jacuzzi overlooking the rear garden is by Piers Gough, suggesting an inverted dome by Borromini (1599–1667); it was one of a number of collaborations with architects and designers.

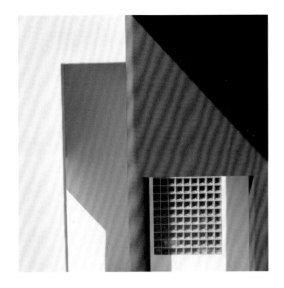

BAGGY HOUSE
CROYDE, NORTH DEVON
Hudson Architects (1994)

There are countless benefits and delights that come from the UK's island status. The sea has always played an important part in the evolution of the country's character and history, including the traditions of coastal living and the waterside house. During the twentieth and twenty-first centuries, this tradition has been updated and revisited many times over and expressed in houses as diverse and wide ranging as Marcel Breuer's Sea Lane House on the Sussex coast (see p. 61), Team 4's Creek Vean in Cornwall (see p. 127) and Future Systems' Malator in Pembrokeshire (see p. 177).

Architect Anthony Hudson (b. 1955) has been repeatedly drawn to the sea, particularly the coastline of Norfolk, the county in which his practice is based, but also the Channel Islands and the West Country. In the early 1990s, he was asked to create a new seaside home on the north Devon coast, known as Baggy House, which became a landmark in his career as well as offering a highly original reinterpretation of a familiar ideal. Hudson elaborates:

The site is exceptional. It's elevated on the cliffs with panoramic views of the Atlantic. The promontory was chosen in the nineteenth century as the site for a house by the founder of the *Birmingham Post*, and later on the house became a hotel. The present owners bought the hotel with the intention of turning it back into a house but it had little architectural merit and the living spaces had no views of the sea. It was decided early on to build anew.

Connecting the new house with the sea vista was one of the most vital aspects of the project, which – in many other respects – came with a relatively open brief. Baggy House needed to provide accommodation for a couple with three children, as well as occasional guests, but Hudson's clients were open minded about the form and aesthetic of the new house. Such latitude allowed Hudson the opportunity to explore fresh ideas while referencing sources of inspiration as diverse as Andrea Palladio's Villa La Rotonda (1590s), Adolf Loos's Villa Müller (1930), Islamic domestic architecture

Below Key family spaces face the sea and forge a direct and vivid link with the open vista. A projecting copper-clad roof canopy helps to protect the adjoining terraces.

Opposite The dining room features a retractable wall of glass, which disappears to create a seamless relationship with the view over the water.

and Pliny's description of his own villa on the Tyrrhenian coast, with its welcoming rooms that not only provide 'a splendid retreat in bad weather' but also 'command the whole expanse of sea and stretch of shore'.[23]

Given the gales that often ravage this part of the Devon coast, balancing the need for shelter and the desire for direct contact with the surroundings became the most pressing challenge in the design of the new house. Its position on the promontory meant that the building could effectively turn its back to the north and open itself up to the south and the sea. Garaging, service spaces and many

amenities, along with the main entrance, sit within a three-storey composition, rendered and crisply painted white, that holds certain echoes – as seen from the driveway – of Charles Rennie Mackintosh (see p. 27) and the work of Arts and Crafts masters such as Charles Voysey (see p. 39).

Yet the house opens up dramatically on the southern elevation, where a retractable wall of glass under a copper-clad canopy is all that separates the 'sea room' and adjoining dining room from the terrace alongside them. Hudson took advantage of the rugged topography of the site to create multiple shifts in level, as seen in the mezzanine living room towards the centre

of the plan that looks across the dining room to the sea. Four bedrooms are arranged at mid-level, with two more in the top-floor tower.

For the interiors, the architect and his clients embraced the use of colour, providing a contrast with the white-rendered walls of the exterior. The same is true of the pool terrace, where a pink bookend wall has the look of the work of Luis Barragán (1902–1988). Here, too, shelter and openness are delicately balanced.

Since Baggy House, Hudson has worked with the same clients on other projects and has also returned to the coast on a number of occasions. In 2016, the practice won the RIBA South East

Regional Award for its work on Le Petit Fort, a new house situated on the shoreline of St Ouen's Bay in Jersey. Then, in 2022, the practice completed the much-praised Coast House on the north Norfolk coastline. Each of these projects was designed around specific contexts and programmes, while imaginatively continuing the practice's exploration of modern coastal living.

CRESCENT HOUSE
MARLBOROUGH DOWNS, WILTSHIRE
Ken Shuttleworth (1997)

The Crescent House could be described as a statement of intent as much as a bespoke country home for Ken Shuttleworth (b. 1952) and his family. It was a personal project completed in the run-up to establishing his own practice, Make, and set the tone for much of the architect's subsequent work. More than anything, the house encapsulates a rejection of the 'modern box' in favour of an architectural approach that is more dynamic, fluid, adaptable and sustainable. This home, in the Wiltshire countryside, offered Shuttleworth an opportunity to explore these ideas and for his wife Seana and their children to serve as the client.

'We are suspicious of modern boxes dumped on unsuspecting landscapes,' says Shuttleworth. 'The building has to feel totally "of" its location. The simple form of the house reacts strongly with the location, reflecting the various contrasts of the site. The critical ingredients are a variety of space related to their function, a response to the changing quality of natural light and sensory contact with nature and the changing seasons.'

Shuttleworth and his family acquired the site in 1994, while the architect was still working at Foster + Partners. The 5-acre parcel of land was part of a former farmstead, which had largely been used for sheep grazing but was occupied by a poorly built house dating from the 1920s with no foundations, plus a few semi-derelict outbuildings. One of the greatest assets of the location was its views of the surrounding landscape, with a vista over the grazing meadows towards the Marlborough Downs and the White Horse that Shuttleworth wanted to make the most of in his design of Crescent House.

The architect created a house consisting of two conjoined crescents, with a double-height hallway running between them. The enclosed crescent to the rear turns its back on neighbouring houses and the nearby access road, while cradling a sequence of family bedrooms and bathrooms. These largely night-time spaces are top-lit, with focused views of the sky rather than the landscape. The other crescent, in complete contrast, is essentially a single space looking

The communal family living spaces sit within a fluid, open-plan sequence facing the gardens, while the central gallery-style hallway serves as both a circulation space and a junction point with the bedrooms and bathrooms to the rear of the building.

out to the open landscape through a curvaceous wall of floor-to-ceiling glass.

The centre point of this great room holds a seating area from which to enjoy the views, as well as a fireplace right at the heart of the plan where the spinal hallway dramatically opens out into the light-filled crescent. A custom kitchen and a dining area sit at one end of this space while a library is situated at the other, with a series of sight lines across the garden and out to the landscape all carefully mapped.

The exterior and interior walls are painted a crisp white, while colour notes are introduced by the choice of art and a rotating set of textiles and ceramics that change according to the season, from blue to yellow to green to red. Such an approach fits with the ambition to create a home that both connects with and responds to seasonal changes in the surrounding landscape, particularly within the 24m-long communal space, which seems to extend its reach outwards

Opposite The kitchen and dining area connects with the central seating zone, beyond which is the study/library at the far end of the open-plan part of the house.

Above The central hallway is illuminated by a continuous ribbon of clerestory windows, while the sequence of family bedrooms beyond sits within the more enclosed section of the building to the rear.

to embrace its setting. Sustainability was another major concern from the start, with Shuttleworth ensuring high standards of insulation and making the most of the warmth of solar gain in the winter months, along with the gradual introduction of green energy solutions.

Winning a great deal of praise and attention on its completion, Crescent House was one of the first of a fresh generation of contemporary country houses that sought to work with the landscape rather than simply impose themselves on it. For Shuttleworth, Crescent House also proved a key point of transition from his time with Foster + Partners to the formal foundation of Make in 2004. The practice has grown

exponentially over the years and has built an international portfolio of work, which – like his own home – has often been infused with an expressive, sculptural character. The house has also become, of course, a much-loved rural retreat for the architect and his family.

'I don't think that building your own house is the sort of thing you should do too young,' Shuttleworth once said. 'It takes time to assess how, and where, you feel you need to live. By the time I finally got round to it, I was married with two children. What my wife Seana and I wanted was a house that would be spacious, airy, bathed in light, yet utilitarian and functional. And strongly rooted in its site.'[24]

MALATOR
DRUIDSTON, PEMBROKESHIRE
Future Systems (1998)

Opposite The most visible element of Malator is the glass eye that faces the sea. This curvaceous wall of glazing is punctuated by a series of small porthole windows that can be opened for ventilation.

Above The house is gently tucked into the coastal landscape with the hillside carried over the building; the carefully considered use of glazing to front and back creates a degree of transparency at the centre of the structure.

Malator is the soul of discretion. Sunk into a hillside where the meadow grass carries over its roof, the house is almost invisible within the Pembrokeshire coastal landscape. From the nearby cliff paths only a rounded lens can be seen, rather like an eye gazing out to sea, with few outward signs of domesticity. Designed by Jan Kaplický (1937–2009) and Amanda Levete (b. 1955) of Future Systems for Bob and Gill Marshall-Andrews, Malator was also one of the most influential houses of the 1990s.

'When I was at the Bar, I frequently used to come here to work and write. It's a wonderful place to work, it really is, and for two reasons,' says Bob Marshall-Andrews (b. 1944), who has enjoyed careers as a barrister, politician and author. 'Firstly, it's quiet and sublime, while the view is lovely. But, secondly, there is nothing much to do. The house is very small, with no clutter apart from books, and the garden is just a riot of wild flowers. It's very difficult to object to a wild flower house.'

The couple have known this part of Wales for around fifty years, sharing a cottage here with friends for many years and celebrating family milestones in a hotel not far from Malator. The owners of the hotel mentioned that a former Nissen-hut-turned-cottage nearby was up for sale and, enchanted by the setting, the Marshall-Andrewses decided to buy it, even though it was in a poor condition.

'We were very fond of it, but then it gradually fell apart,' recalls Bob. 'It was on the brink and then our son Tom, who was a student at the time, simply sketched out an idea for a circular building on a piece of paper.' Gill continues:

Then my mother saw an article in the newspaper about Future Systems, who were just building their Glass House [also known as the Hauer-King House, 1994] in London. So we contacted them and brought them down. It was February, blowing a gale, and there was also a dead whale down on the beach. I can remember walking up the path with Jan and stopping near the top and saying that the house has got to sink into the landscape. The footprint could be no bigger than the footprint of the original hut and the local

planners said it couldn't be built of brick or stone. That was the brief and this is what they came up with.

The soft shapes and rounded contours of Malator, which was named after the former hut on the site, sat well within the context of other sculptural projects by Future Systems such as the Media Centre at Lord's Cricket Ground (1999) and Selfridges in Birmingham (2003). Yet there was also an innate sense of modesty to the house, which held three bedrooms in the wings and an open-plan living area at its centre. The couple asked for just two changes to the original plans, which were the introduction of a circular fireplace in the living area, flanked by a sofa facing the sea view, and then a larger expanse of glass around the main entrance to the rear,

Left The centre of the house is open plan, with a bespoke kitchen, a dining zone and a seating area – the focus throughout is on the framed panorama of the sea.

Below The semicircular fitted sofa faces the water and the central fireplace; the Marshall-Andrewses requested that the hearth was situated at the heart of the plan.

Below The bathrooms, utility room and kitchen sit within two prefabricated pods that were delivered to the site as completed units; they also divide the central living area from the bedrooms in the wings.

Opposite The master bedroom is spacious enough for a study area with a fitted desk and shelves; an additional two bedrooms are situated in the opposite wing of the house.

which allows for a degree of transparency right through the house.

Kaplický and Levete also designed two prefabricated pods, one holding the bathroom and a galley kitchenette while the other hosted a shower and utility space. Delivered to site ready made and craned in, these pods help separate the central living area from the bedrooms in the wings. Beyond the bookcases in the master bedroom, which also serves as a study, there is very little storage space in the house, requiring the couple to adopt a relatively minimal and uncluttered lifestyle at Malator.

Given its position within the Pembrokeshire Coast National Park, the house was momentarily controversial. Yet its discretion and respect

for the landscape soon made it an exemplar in terms of building a contemporary home within areas of natural beauty and significance, while the model of submergence was later adopted in other rural projects. The house was nicknamed the 'Teletubby House', after the hobbit-like home occupied by the beloved characters on the children's television show. It's a name that the Marshall-Andrewses soon came to love. 'It helped to warm people to the house,' Gill says, 'which replaced something that was rather tatty and falling down.'

'And the planners loved it and they still do,' adds Bob. 'They regard it as being an accolade for the Park, rather than otherwise, and I think they are right.'

SKYWOOD HOUSE
DENHAM, MIDDLESEX
Graham Phillips (1999)

There were three important points of inspiration that influenced the design of Graham Phillips's Skywood House. The first was Mies van der Rohe's Barcelona Pavilion (1929), particularly the master architect's use of the pinwheel plan, as well as the dissolution of the barriers between inside and outside space. The second was the work of Mexican architect Luis Barragán (1902–1988), especially his use of high walls to enclose courtyards and outdoor rooms. The third was the gardens of Kyoto, which Phillips (b. 1947) visited while working on the HSBC building (1986) during his years at Foster + Partners. Phillips elaborates:

> Visiting the Kyoto gardens was one of the biggest eureka moments for me and realizing that with architecture the integration of building and landscape need to be considered as a totality. I didn't try to recreate a Japanese garden here, because we had all these oak trees and rhododendrons, but we did try and enhance the British landscape around us and respond to it. The other thing with those Japanese gardens was that the relationship with water was fundamental, so creating a lake here in front of the house was very important to us.

While based in Hong Kong, Phillips began thinking about designing and building a home for himself, his wife and their children. He was with Foster + Partners for thirty-five years, eventually becoming chief executive, but the house was undertaken as a personal project when the family returned to London. Having managed major projects like the HSBC building and Chek Lap Kok Airport (1998), Skywood offered Phillips an opportunity to work on something more personal and at a more intimate scale, while he savoured the opportunity to get back to the drawing board. 'I had made up my mind that I wanted to design and build a house, which very few architects that I had known had ever done,' Phillips says. 'One of the problems with a blank sheet of paper project for architects, like a house, is that you know you are going to be judged. But perhaps I wasn't as self-conscious as other people and decided to go ahead with it.'

After searching for a suitable site for some years, Phillips eventually came across a 4½-acre woodland plot within the Middlesex greenbelt, complete with a dilapidated chalet bungalow suitable for replacement. The first task was to clear the gardens of fallen trees, which had been brought down by the 'great storm' of 1987, and begin surveying the remaining woodland, which was carefully preserved. The new house was built close to the position of the old bungalow it replaced, with just a 20 per cent increase allowed to the footprint by the local planning authority.

Phillips suggests that these limitations were, ultimately, beneficial, leading to a single-storey house of a relatively modest size but with an imaginative design that gives the impression of generosity and open space. The approach to the house carries you around the lake before guiding you into a partly walled entrance courtyard towards the rear of the building.

Left The spacious, open-plan living area connects with the adjoining terrace and enjoys views over the lake, which is bordered by mature trees.

Below The great room includes the kitchen, dining area and seating zone, all sitting within this glass-sided pavilion floating in the landscape.

Opposite Integrated storage and fitted furniture, including the kitchen units, help to liberate the living spaces and preserve the clean lines of the house, while the gardens, planting and water pools provide constant connections to the natural world and changing seasons.

Above The bedroom wing ends with the master suite that overlooks the courtyard garden and swimming pool; this semi-enclosed setting offers privacy and allows for idyllic indulgences such as the corner bath by the window.

The main entrance sits at the junction between two wings. The master pavilion on one side holds the open-plan living area, including the dining zone and the kitchen to the rear, and spills out onto a terrace overlooking the lake. The family bedrooms are contained within the second wing, which pushes out in the opposite direction, offering views of a more private and partially enclosed garden to the rear.

Later, Phillips added a swimming pool and converted a garage into a guest annexe, creating a third pavilion. Integrated storage walls throughout and hidden service spaces ensure that Skywood remains uncluttered, while the eye is constantly drawn to the water and the surrounding landscape. He concludes:

In a way, you don't need decoration of art on the walls, because the richness is within this landscape, which we have brought inside. The glass boxes of the bedroom wing face east for the morning sun while the living [area] faces west for the evening sun, so you have this L-shaped pair of walls and then the frameless glass, which disappears so that you feel like you are sitting in the landscape. Then wonderful things begin to happen which I never even envisaged to be honest...the deer and the foxes come up and push their noses right against the glass. These are things that you don't think about when you are designing, but it's just magical.

THE BLACK HOUSE
PRICKWILLOW, CAMBRIDGESHIRE
Meredith Bowles (2004)

Opposite On the edge of an open field, this tall, dark dwelling stands out vividly against the sky. The former studio to the front of the house now holds a spacious family living room.

Above The house is gently elevated on its Fenland site, with a form and choice of materials that reference the agricultural sheds and barns of the region.

Living in The Black House, says architect Meredith Bowles (b. 1963), is rather like being inside a giant sun dial. The house itself sits on the edge of a small Cambridgeshire village and looks across the Fens towards the towers of Ely Cathedral in the far distance. The combination of a wide open landscape and the big skies means that the changing pattern of the day, from sunrise to sunset, can be keenly felt, as well as the changing seasons.

'It's great to feel the world turning,' says Bowles, who shares the house with his wife, novelist Jill Dawson, and their grown-up children. 'It is a great spot and I know exactly where the sun will set at different times of the year. I love the utilitarian, unpretentious nature of the landscape, which is not "pretty" but tough and it has to deal with the wind and the water. It has really affected the way that I think about things and has influenced my work.'

Bowles and Dawson did not know the Fens before decamping from Hackney to Cambridgeshire. However, they soon fell in love with their surroundings, while the proximity to Cambridge, where Bowles's architectural practice is based, has always been an important factor. On a day out to see a pair of architect-designed houses in the village, they spotted a parcel of land for sale that sat alongside an open field. Bowles seized the opportunity to design and build a family home from scratch, while based in a rented farmhouse nearby.

The site and setting were pivotal in the design process, with Bowles opting for a tall, three-storey, timber-framed building raised on modest piers. This solution not only made the most of the open views and provided the family with the spaces it needed, but also dealt with drainage issues related to the way that the land there is slowly sinking below the level of the roads and their service channels. The corrugated black coating of the highly insulated house also draws inspiration from the agricultural sheds and barns that punctuate the land. Bowles says:

Because the area is so flat, the buildings do stick out like dice rolled on a flat surface. The pitch-roofed houses and barns do assume very simple forms, which is characteristic of the area,

Below and opposite The former studio has been linked to the main house with the addition of a new morning room, which has become one of Bowles's favourite spaces on account of its mesmerizing views across the open, agricultural landscape.

and often you find that there is nothing much else around them. So that was the starting point really. Then if you are working with timber it makes sense to raise the building off the ground to get some ventilation coming through, and the dark coat is not only an echo of the barns painted in pitch but also the freshly ploughed furrows of the field, where the earth is this rich, velvety black colour.

During the early days of his practice, Mole Architects, Bowles worked from a room in the house, while Dawson occupied an attic study at the top of The Black House. But as the practice grew and won more commissions – ranging from housing to university buildings and cultural projects – Bowles decided to build a separate, single-storey studio alongside the house on the edge of the field. Eventually, Mole outgrew the studio as well, so the practice moved to larger offices in Cambridge, and Bowles began to think about reclaiming the studio for himself and the family as well as connecting it to the house. Bowles explains:

There were a few years when the studio was just sitting here and being used as a

Below The architectural studio has been repurposed as an inviting sitting room, complete with a wood-burning stove; it provides a generously scaled alternative to the original living room in the main house.

Opposite The design of the ground-floor kitchen and the adjoining living room makes the most of the open views towards Ely Cathedral in the far distance, with integrated ingredients such as the window seat looking across the fields.

store room, partly because I was thinking about the best way of connecting it to the house in a way that would feel right. So eventually we designed this link through to a new morning room, which has been extraordinary really. It faces south and has opened up the whole house for us in a way that was quite unexpected. So this little room, which I had started off thinking about just as a way of getting from one place to another, has actually ended up getting a huge amount of use and has become a favourite spot.

The studio itself was converted into a spacious new living room, complete with a wood-burning

stove and seating that benefits from the field views. Yet any changes to the master building have been very limited, reflecting the successful nature of the original design, with The Black House becoming a 'forever home' for both Bowles and Dawson, who continues to work and write in her attic retreat.

'The feeling of wanting to write really comes from where I am, but I do also need privacy and a quiet place to work where I feel unobserved,' says Dawson. 'The Black House does have this sense of being enclosed and when I'm up at the top I feel tucked away and safe. But then there are the views, so you also feel part of this huge, open space. To me, that's the genius of Meredith's design.'

PENCALENICK HOUSE
FOWEY ESTUARY, CORNWALL
Seth Stein Architects (2006)

Opposite The use of natural materials and the decision to gently push the new house into the hillside gives Pencalenick an organic architectural quality.

Above The hillside position offers views over the River Fowey while the mature trees around the site help to soften the visual impact of the building.

The setting of Pencalenick House is, as architect Seth Stein (b. 1959) puts it, 'very *Swallows & Amazons*'. This site-sensitive home overlooks the estuary of the River Fowey in Cornwall, along with its collection of moored boats, while also being surrounded by a forest of oak trees to the point that the building almost disappears into the woods. The house only reveals itself by degrees as you arrive by boat and reach the diagonal stone jetty pointing up the sloping shoreline. The same is true when you approach by road, with the green-roofed house remaining almost invisible until the very last moment.

'When you arrive by car you go down all these narrow Cornish lanes, like a toboggan running down these green tubes with high hedges either side,' explains Stein. 'And then you approach through the forest and see a small portion of the building, which is just a stone wall and the roof is grassed over, so there's very little that denotes arrival. It is rather enigmatic.'

This gradual process of discovery only accentuates the sense of anticipation as Pencalenick finally begins to reveal itself. The way that the two-storey building has been

gently pushed into the hillside means that the main entrance on the lower level is reached via a set of stone steps leading downwards, with the view across the water unfolding along the way.

'Fowey itself is very pretty so it's rather nice to be opposite, looking over the estuary with all the boats bobbing around and then the picturesque town behind it,' Stein says. 'The house sits within its own 4-acre plot of woodland and the land beyond it is owned by the National Trust. So you really are nestling among a forest.'

Stein's client at Pencalenick wanted to commission a contextual but contemporary family home, suited to holiday use but that would also accommodate visitors and guests with ease. The site itself was once occupied by a Victorian isolation hospital, but little of this remained beyond remnants and ruins by the time Seth Stein Architects started work on the project. Yet there was a clear precedent for a building on what had become an unkempt site and a desire to restore the landscape around it.

'The planning process itself was positive and the local planners were pleased to see a contemporary house here within a process of

Opposite and above The seating and dining areas form a double-height reception room at the heart of the house. The focal point fireplace is set within a stone wall that extends out towards the terrace in line with the boat ramp down to the water; the upstairs landing acts as a bridge spanning the space.

regeneration,' remembers Stein. 'We did do some analysis on what the impact might be of any glazing and possible light pollution while looking at integrating the house with the landscape.'

The house includes six bedrooms and generously scaled living spaces, yet remains a discreet presence within its surroundings. Stein pushed the gently curving, two-storey building into the slope of the hill with a retaining wall to the rear and a long line of circulation running alongside it, top-lit by a skylight set into the green roof. The majority of the family bedrooms and bathrooms are on the upper floor, although two are on the lower-ground level. Here, Stein designed a

double-height living area around a focal point fireplace, with an angled surround sitting in line with the stone jetty that runs down to the water.

In terms of materials, Stein and his clients purposefully opted for largely natural and textural materials. Apart from the concrete retaining wall, the rest of the building is timber framed and features extensive use of elm for the floors and integrated, bespoke joinery. Stonework is used both outside and in, as seen in the fireplace wall, which extends outwards to help frame and define the terrace that adjoins the living area.

'There is some lovely stonework using local slate, which we were really happy about as it enabled us to use local craftsmen. It

Above The gentle curve of the façade creates a more natural form in this wooded setting, while the timber shutters and detailing add to the crafted character of the house.

Opposite A top-lit, spinal corridor runs along the back of the building linking the enfilade of sleeping spaces on the upper storey, where the elevated bedrooms and bathrooms look over the tree canopy.

gives another quality to the house,' elaborates Stein. 'And when you are dealing with sitting rooms in houses with amazing views, like this, then you want to reconcile the idea of looking outwards with arranging the room around the fireplace. We wanted to combine the two, so the element of the hearth is quite emotive here and very much the symbol of the home.'

One of the most engaging elements of Pencalenick is the way that the vista across the water is present from almost every living space in the house. The upstairs bedrooms, in particular, also look across the tree canopy, lending these rooms something of a seductive

treehouse character. The sense of tranquillity provided by connecting with nature so intimately is palpable.

'It's just such a fantastic site and the building is so calm,' says Stein. 'And the house creates so much interest through some very simple ideas. It's also satisfying to see how it has weathered, with the timber turning silver but the stonework looking as good as it always has. There's no doubt that when you go to Pencalenick it feels very special.'

HOLMEWOOD HOUSE
MARLOW, BUCKINGHAMSHIRE
Robin Partington (2007)

Opposite The gentle curves and contours of the house work in concert with the topography of the landscape itself, with an intricate and sensitive relationship established between architecture and nature.

Above The carefully choreographed approach to Holmewood means that the house only reveals itself late in the journey through the estate and, even then, by degrees, all adding to the sense of arrival.

Situated within the open meadows of a Chilterns estate, Holmewood almost disappears into its pastoral setting. This is a twenty-first-century country house of substance and scale, yet it nestles quietly in the gentle folds of the landscape, with a green roof that stretches the length of the building. It is a home that reveals itself only by degrees, remaining almost invisible until the very last moment, yet the interiors are full of light and lifted by a vivid relationship with their surroundings.

'It sits on an 150-acre estate, including 50 acres of beech woods. Because it's in an area of outstanding natural beauty it had to be sensitively inserted into the landscape,' says architect Robin Partington (b. 1960). 'But there is no sense that you are underground at all. Yes, the building is an integral part of the landscape and, yes, the roof does have a lawnmower that goes over the top of it. But once you are inside there is no sense of being in a bunker or a cave. It is very airy and light.'

The house was commissioned by patron of the arts, designer and philanthropist Lady Helen Hamlyn (b. 1934), to serve as a private,

rural retreat. With her late husband, publisher Paul Hamlyn (1926–2001), Lady Hamlyn used to live in a seventeenth-century country house in Gloucestershire. But eventually the couple started to think about building a contemporary, bespoke home for themselves closer to London and began searching for a suitable site. It was a project that Lady Hamlyn decided to continue after Lord Hamlyn passed away in 2001, working closely with Robin Partington on the design of Holmewood. Their original proposal for a house above ground – partly inspired by botanist Mary Eleanor Bowes's (1749–1800) orangery at Gibside in the northeast of England – was turned down by the local planners, which led to a radical reworking of the plans. Partington remembers:

We had actually started working out how the rooms in the house would relate to one another and how Lady Hamlyn's furniture would go into these rooms. So we thought of simply taking a scalpel to the landscape and lifting it up like a duvet and sliding in Lady Hamlyn's diagram of how she wanted to live and that is exactly what we have

Opposite The central part of the house is devoted to key circulation routes and a pool with an adjustable floor that can be raised when required to create a generously scaled reception room.

Below A carefully curated selection of art and antiques stands out against a gentle palette of colour tones and textures for the walls and floors.

now. We went back to the planners and having initially said, 'never in a million years', they said the new idea was fantastic. The planners were incredibly supportive and helpful.

Lady Hamlyn was very clear from the outset about the programme for the house, wanting a sequence of neatly ordered spaces arranged around a central axis. The driveway through the beech woods leads to the crescent-shaped entrance area, partly protected by the landscaping around the house, which recycled some of the excavated soil and chalk while the remainder was reused by local farmers. A welcoming entrance hall leads through to a central atrium, top-lit by a skylight, with a

pool; at the touch of a button the floor of the pool begins to rise and the water drains away to transform the space into a large reception room.

Bedrooms and bathrooms are arranged on either side of this central axis, but sit beyond integrated foyers that help to ensure privacy while avoiding the need for multiple doorways along this key route through the house. At the far end of the building, the living room and dining area are flanked by the kitchen to one side and the master suite to the other, with all of these spaces benefiting from a gently curving wall of floor-to-ceiling glass looking out over the pasture and woodland beyond, as well as connecting with an adjoining terrace.

High ceilings enhance the sense of openness, with natural light circulating throughout the

Below The sitting room enjoys open views over the landscape through a floor-to-ceiling wall of glass, while the adjoining terrace and reflecting pool form a hinterland between the interior and the surroundings.

Opposite The layout of the house provides a sensitive balance between more open spaces, such as the sitting room, and the private realm of bedrooms and bathrooms, which are carefully positioned to maximize privacy while still connecting to the landscape.

house. The choice of materials, finishes and detailing creates an elegant backdrop for Lady Hamlyn's curated collection of furniture, art and tapestries.

'The detailing is very minimal but there is a lot of technology behind the scenes,' says Partington. 'The whole idea of the house was that it was a neutral foil for the things that then went into it. There are gallery-like qualities but it still feels warm and welcoming.'

Holmewood is a site-specific solution fully tailored to the landscape and the requirements of its owner. The house is an architectural exemplar in terms of

creating a twenty-first-century country home in a sensitive rural setting, yet Holmewood is also very much a home, layered with character and individuality.

'It's exactly what I knew it would be,' states Lady Hamlyn. 'I never start a building unless I can see it absolutely finished in my mind and the rooms were designed around the antiques, which needed to breathe and be enjoyed. You can see how it sits so beautifully in the countryside and we were extremely lucky that the land faces, more or less, south and downhill. It is a very peaceful house.'

ORIGAMI HOUSE

BALLYMENA, COUNTY ANTRIM

Jane Burnside (2008)

The garden and grounds around Jane Burnside's home are extraordinarily verdant, even at the height of summer. There are giant gunneras and super-sized hostas, bordered by mature trees, creating a lush, green backdrop against which the crisp, white outline of Origami House stands out vividly. It is, in part, the stream – or burn – that runs alongside the house that makes the gardens so fertile, while also providing a natural border between the driveway and the private domain of the residence itself. A bridge across the water forms part of the processional entrance sequence, with the soothing sound of the water ever present.

'When my children were small and we lived in the farmhouse nearby, we used to come over here and have a picnic because it was so peaceful by the water,' recalls Burnside (b. 1965). 'It was always lovely, although the day that we moved in to the new house there was a storm with the water running a foot over the dam. The noise was terrifying but I had carefully worked out all my levels, so it passed the flood test.'

Sitting close to a rural village to the south of Ballymena, the house is composed of a series of interlinked pavilions arranged on a single level but with multiple shifts in scale and volume. The zig-zag roofline of Origami House gives the building its name, while the way that the pavilions frame the views across the surrounding landscape ensures an engaging indoor–outdoor relationship.

Shared with her grown-up sons and her husband, architect-turned-artist David Page, Burnside's home is one of the most eloquent and accomplished expressions of the architect's response to the 'problem of the Northern Irish bungalow'. Growing frustrated with the regional preoccupation with traditional bungalows, complete with their neo-classical Georgian detailing, Burnside began thinking about a fresh approach that drew on her studies in Manchester, Bath and the British School at Rome, as well as her time working in America with architects such as Michael Graves. Rejecting the established model, Burnside began reinventing the 'bungalow' as a contemporary home composed of a series of repeated modules.

'In Northern Ireland you have these little groupings of cottages in the countryside called

Below and opposite The main living spaces and the kitchen are located at the centre of a free-flowing plan, with high ceilings, banks of glass and fluid connections with the terraces and garden all adding to the sense of openness.

"clachans",' says Burnside. 'They usually grew up around farms and were little more than 6 m wide and whitewashed. So I started thinking about that kind of combination of structures with an open-plan layout. Using these small modules of around 6 m or so gives you some of the feeling and scale of those old Irish cottages.'

Burnside refined the design of these repeated modules over a number of projects, with Origami House being the third in the sequence. Having acquired such a tempting site alongside her former home, Burnside created a new family residence composed of six interlinked pavilions, while a seventh nearby now serves as a painting studio for her husband.

From the main entrance there is a choice of either entering Burnside's office, where she

bases her practice, or stepping through into the family's private realm. In the latter, the first impression is of space, volume and light with a fluid layout for the main living spaces and easy connections with the adjoining terraces overlooking the front garden. There is a natural progression through to the master suite at the far end of the house, while additional bedrooms for Burnside's sons and guests sit towards the rear of the house. These can easily be separated off if not in use, creating flexibility in terms of daily patterns of living. Burnside elucidates:

It was about using this modular system and refining the details to create these different shapes for the pavilions. You have the light and the views, but inside you can

Opposite The combination of extensive fenestration and large skylights ensures spaces that are filled with sunlight, while more private zones such as the master bedroom connect naturally with the terraces and gardens.

Below The repeated forms and pitched roofs of the pavilions create an engaging rhythm; the tall chimneys punctuate the sawtooth roofline.

carve bits out of them and use the shapes to define the spaces, so the kitchen area has its own little roof over it and the same with the dining area, but the seating area is this big volume. When you come inside the house everything starts to open up and you get this embrace of the landscape.

The mature trees around the house were carefully preserved during the landscaping process, while horticulturalist Keith Crawford advised on the planting around the winding stream. Together, they help to both frame and soften the graphic outline of this sculptural and characterful twenty-first-century bungalow.

KENT RESERVOIR HOUSE

HARRIETSHAM, KENT
Brinkworth (2011)

Opposite The new house is arranged on two storeys. The reworked reservoir tank holds the majority of the family living spaces and bedrooms at ground-floor level, while a new glass pavilion upstairs forms an open-plan lounge, library, study and belvedere.

Above The project started by uncovering and revealing the bunker-like concrete reservoir before beginning the process of converting the water tank into a home.

The creation of Kent Reservoir House was an archaeological process as much as an architectural challenge. The project began with the discovery of a redundant reservoir tank sitting within an idyllic rural location overlooking the North Downs, one of two original reservoirs built during the 1930s by the local water board. This bucolic bunker had been put up for auction and was spotted by architectural designer Kevin Brennan (b. 1967) of Brinkworth, who thought the building might appeal to two of his clients: artist Dinos Chapman (b. 1962) and knitwear designer Tiphaine de Lussy (b. 1963).

'Kevin rang while we were away and told us that he had found this concrete box and we should take a look at it,' remembers Chapman. 'I said that we should just get it, because I wanted a project, and so I first saw it after we bought it. When we came to see it, it was strange; I couldn't believe how big it was. The experience of going into this old, disused reservoir was quite amazing.'

Fortunately, a good deal of trust between architect and clients had already been established with an earlier project. Both

Chapman and de Lussy were confident that Brinkworth would bring the building to life and convert it successfully into a family home. This process began with scraping away the banks of earth that surrounded the former tank, which had been designed to hold 500,000 gallons of water. Uncovering this 'monumental' structure allowed its original character to reveal itself, while also beginning to suggest the way in which the rigorous grid of the superstructure might be adapted and extended.

'It might seem brave now, but at the time it just seemed like this is it, this is perfect, and we knew it would work out,' explains de Lussy. 'We had already worked with Kevin and we trusted him, but he also learnt to understand what works for us. When they dug away the earth it was very exciting, because you could suddenly see the concrete and it looked beautiful.'

All agreed on the need to preserve as much of the character of the raw concrete as possible. Brinkworth developed a plan for the house based on the formal grid provided by the tank itself, carving openings and apertures to the front of the building to connect the main living

Above and opposite The main family living spaces are all interconnected, with the kitchen at one end, the dining area at the centre and a seating zone arranged around the fireplace at the other end. They all sit within part of the old reservoir that leads out to a terrace and offers open connections with the surroundings. The large painting is by Peter Halley (b. 1953).

spaces with the views via banks of floor-to-ceiling glass. This communal family zone was kept as open as possible, with a seating area created around a new fireplace with a brick surround at one end, a dining area in the centre and a bespoke kitchen at the opposite end. The original pillars and ceilings remained exposed, complemented by polished concrete floors and white render for the internal partition walls that separate the space from the rest of the house.

To the rear, Brennan designed a linear sequence of five bedrooms that overlooks a sunken rear courtyard inhabited by a slim swimming pool. The courtyard doubles as a lightwell, drawing sunlight deep into the interiors, with the water helping to reflect the light and provide a calm, soothing backdrop. A studio, services and circulation spaces are also arranged on this lower level.

By way of contrast, Brinkworth added a 'Mies-like glass and steel pavilion' on top of the concrete box. This is an open studio-style space, serving multiple purposes from living room to library to gallery to belvedere. It is

Above The bedrooms and bathrooms form an enfilade running towards the rear of the house and looking across the swimming pool that inhabits the courtyard carved out to one side of the former reservoir.

Opposite The way that the bedrooms connect with the pool courtyard ensures a rich quality of natural light, while the fixtures and furnishings mix bespoke elements with mid-century designs by Charles and Ray Eames, George Nelson and others.

an ideal spot for appreciating the open views across the surrounding landscape, while the overhanging roof provides a degree of shade and shelter for the interiors and also for part of the adjoining roof terrace.

Brennan's approach to the conversion of the reservoir not only created an original, inventive and characterful rural home, but also offers an exemplar of creative, adaptive reuse. It was a design philosophy that his clients were delighted to embrace, seeing it as well attuned to their own interests in architecture and design. Chapman concludes:

It is a lovely location and, standing on top of it, looking out, the countryside

looks really beautiful. But it was the building that I was more interested in, and I have always liked concrete. With the first walk around the reservoir it felt cavernous and huge, but it didn't feel like a living space. It was a big, empty resounding box. For Kevin to see the potential in that was the genius behind the project, and his imagination was the driving force behind it. It was all about what you do with the space.

LITTLE COTTAGE
PRAA SANDS, CORNWALL
Alex Michaelis (2011)

For architect Alex Michaelis (b. 1965), the design of his family homes has offered golden opportunities to explore fresh ideas that have in turn informed his wider work. This includes the Round House, in west London, where Michaelis developed an imaginative solution to the challenges of an urban infill site. Then there is Little Cottage (2012), in Cornwall, where Michaelis and his partner, art consultant Susanna Bell, were seduced by an extraordinary coastal site and welcomed the chance to create an escapist, modern home that combines sculptural forms with an emphasis on sustainable living. The project began after a good friend encouraged them to take a look at a derelict house overlooking the beach at Praa Sands.

'We drove down to take a look and it was the most amazing site...with these big open skies and 180-degree views out across the sea,' says Michaelis, a founding partner at Michaelis Boyd, which he launched in 1996 with Tim Boyd. 'There was this cottage with some land around it for the same price as a garage in Acton, and the setting was so beautiful. I just couldn't resist it.'

Initially, Michaelis thought it might be possible to reinvent the existing clifftop house. But it soon became clear that the walls of the existing cottage were crumbling away and that the only realistic way forward was to replace it with a new building set further back from the cliff and tucked into the gently sloping site as it rises landward and to the north. Michaelis says:

I camped out here a couple of times before I actually designed the house. The main thing was to make the most of the view, so that even when you are here in the middle of winter and the rain is horizontal against the windows you still get this amazing panorama of the ocean. The spaces have to face southwards to the sea and then it's about working backwards from that to make sure that everything else functions well. That's why we brought out the staircase at the back of the building but with a rounded form like a shell, so I was taking inspiration from the natural elements here and seeing how that might work.

Reference points include Eileen Gray's (1878–1976) E-1027 villa (1929) on the Côte d'Azur, along with other early Modernist buildings such as Erich Mendelsohn (1887–1953) and Serge Chermayeff's (1900–1996) De La Warr Pavilion (1935) in Bexhill-on-Sea. But there was also the example of the Californian Case Study Houses and the work of the New York Five, including Charles Gwathmey (1938–2009) and John Hejduk (1929–2000), particularly in relation to the idea of softening the more linear aspects of the house. While the seaward spaces, both downstairs and

Opposite and below The family living area is free flowing and open plan, with the kitchen, dining area and lounge all enjoying a direct sense of connection with the terrace alongside and the wide-ranging views through the floor-to-ceiling wall of glass.

Above The upstairs landing is top-lit and runs along the rear of the building, linking the main run of family bedrooms and bathrooms, all of which enjoy framed sea views.

Opposite The elevated bedrooms enjoy wide open vistas across the sea, while adopting a soft and soothing tonal palette in keeping with the coastal setting.

upstairs, are arranged in a strong axial line, the funnel-like staircase and other more playful elements define the house's unique character.

'It's the softness of those round forms that I have always loved,' confirms Michaelis. 'I have become rather renowned in the office for doing porthole windows whenever I can, for instance. It's about softening and humanizing the hard edges of modern architecture while still keeping a clear and simple design philosophy.'

Many of the building's structural components were prefabricated and delivered to the site for assembly, while Michaelis introduced an air-source heat pump to feed the underfloor heating and photovoltaic panels for electricity. The main living spaces on the ground floor are largely open plan, benefiting from banks of glass, front

and back, that provide a degree of transparency as well as framing the open vista of the coast. Upstairs, a line of family bedrooms also enjoys the panorama, while a circulation corridor runs to the rear. A sheltered verandah provides an all-weather halfway point between outside and in.

'I love being by the water and have done since the age of ten, when we had a little boat with a tiny motor and we used to go out fishing near Toulon, which is where my dad lives,' says Michaelis. 'I like to just sit at the dining table, looking out at the sea and perhaps doing some work. It's incredibly peaceful and you can get so much done here. It is an incredibly calm space to be in, with the ever-changing sky and ocean. You can sit here forever, just looking out, and getting into this pattern of relaxation.'

COTSWOLDS HOUSE

CRANHAM, GLOUCESTERSHIRE
Richard Found (2012)

Opposite The substantial new addition contrasts with the original cottage in some respects, yet the use of stonework and the way that the buildings sit in the landscape also provides a respectful bond between them.

Above A slim glass link ties the two buildings together while still preserving a subtle sense of separation; at the same time, the new elements are gently woven into the landscape, overlooking the lake and surrounding woodland.

Sitting in a quiet and secluded bowl in the Cotswolds landscape and surrounded by woodland, architect Richard Found's country home presents a striking contrast between the old and the new. A long track winds down through the trees towards an eighteenth-century gamekeeper's cottage and the dramatic twenty-first-century addition alongside it. This is now a spacious family home that Found (b. 1966) shares with his wife, art consultant Jane Suitor, and their two children, with views out across the clearing and down towards the lake. The two structures offer an intriguing conversation between past and present, with a clear distinction made between them. Yet certain points of reference also tie them together.

'It is the dialogue between the old and the new that really makes the project work. It's interesting to see people's reactions when they come here, because it's not what people think of when they come to the Cotswolds,' says Found, whose architectural practice is based in London. 'They are surprised by the fact that there is something so contemporary in such an ancient woodland environment. The effect that it has on people seems to be that they let their hair down and relax, like us, because it almost feels like being on holiday when you are here.'

Found and Suitor first got to know the area on their own family holidays and began looking for a possible getaway in the region. They spotted an advertisement in a local newspaper for the original cottage and its adjoining grounds, which were once part of the local estate. The cottage itself was in need of restoration while the sheds and gardens were in poor condition. Yet Found and his wife instantly saw the potential to create a very special escape. Found continues:

I came down on the first day that the cottage was on the market and instantly fell in love with the plot of land. It hadn't been touched for perhaps sixty years and was very run down, with kitchen gardens, chicken runs, an aviary and derelict outhouses. I put down a deposit there and then because it was all about the privacy and seclusion of the site, which was the total opposite to the frenetic pace of

Below The principal family living spaces sit within one of the two new wings of the house, with a kitchen and dining area connecting with both the living room and the substantial terrace overlooking the landscape.

Right With its walls of glass, the sitting room can serve as a belvedere during the day while the fireplace to the rear of the space comes into its own in the evenings; the ampersand artwork is by Shannon Ebner (b. 1971).

London life. It ticked all the boxes when it came to the landscape, the lake and the secluded feeling of it all.

Initially, Found thought he might want to replace the original cottage with something completely new. But when local planners got wind of the plan they requested spot listing for the cottage, which meant that it could not be demolished. At first this seemed like a major setback, but gradually Found embraced the idea of restoring the original building and adding something fresh alongside it.

'The cottage itself is very quaint and beautiful, but I could see that it was going to be much too small for us as a family. So I totalled up the square footage of the derelict buildings and outhouses and that added up to around 5,000 square feet,' says Found. 'That's how I

Below Outdoor rooms and fresh air spaces have been created around the new elements of the house, including a roof terrace positioned on top of the wing holding the principal living spaces.

Opposite The proportions, materials and aesthetic approach seen in the new wings contrast with the restored interior of the former gamekeeper's cottage, where the exposed beams and original features create a more characterful set of spaces, offering a more intimate way of living.

managed to get permission for this "extension", if you like, and for it being so sizeable. The planners became very excited about it in the end, as they hadn't approved such a contemporary scheme before, and after it won a RIBA award they were even happier.'

While the cottage was sensitively restored and updated, Found decided to gently push the new, single-storey addition into the slope of the hillside, using a structural framework of concrete and steel. Importantly, banks of glass face the open views down towards the lake. The building is clad in local stone, which is also used for the low retaining walls that border the adjoining terraces, helping to form a relationship between the new elements and the two-storey cottage.

A largely open-plan living area is arranged to one side of the main entrance, while the bedrooms run in a neat line in the other direction; a junction of just a few steps distinguishes between these communal and private realms. Integrated storage throughout keeps the spaces uncluttered, while an air-source heat pump serves the underfloor heating, and fireplaces warm both the old and the new zones.

'We love the peace and quiet but also the way that the sun moves around the building during the day,' says Found. 'And it's also interesting how the two parts of the house suit different pastimes. During the day we will be in the new addition, but if I want to read a book I will probably go into the cottage and read by the fire.'

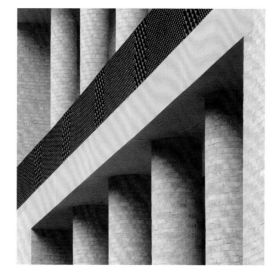
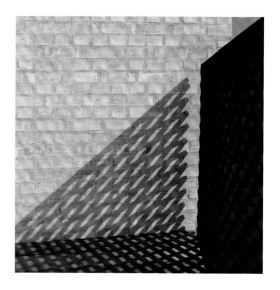

COTTAGE PLACE
KENSINGTON, LONDON
David Chipperfield (2012)

Opposite Although the house is substantial in scale, Cottage Place is also a gentle presence on the streetscape, with its discreet entrance and dual loggia above providing a hinterland between the house and its central London setting.

Above Echoes of an Italianate villa in a modern idiom carry across such details as the repeated columns, the use of characterful materials and the highly crafted quality of the finishes.

British architect David Chipperfield (b. 1953) is best known for his large-scale cultural projects around the world, ranging from the rebuilding of the Neues Museum in Berlin (2009) to the Museo Jumex in Mexico City (2013), and more recent landmarks in his home country, such as Turner Contemporary in Margate and The Hepworth in Wakefield (both 2011). Yet residential projects formed an important strand within his portfolio for many years.

Common threads within this varied output are a particular sense of cohesion and restraint, a respect for context and history, and an engaging fusion of sophistication and simplicity. Yet, at the same time, they are all decidedly twenty-first-century buildings: 'We are trying to make something that's abstract and contemporary on the one hand, but completely inspired by its own task and function,' Chipperfield confirms.

This determination to never resort to established stereotypes or form-giving showmanship has made it difficult to pigeonhole the architect and his work. Yet, Chipperfield's ability to make poetry out of simple, geometrical architecture, as the late Richard Rogers once put

it, and his mastery of programmatic planning, functionality, detailing and finish – even on a large scale – has helped to make him one of the most influential and successful architects of his generation. Another aspect of his buildings that has often been noted is that they are truly 'humane', which is of vital concern when it relates to house and home.

Although this London town house is a substantial dwelling, it always strives to be humane, offering welcome and comfort throughout. It is situated just off Brompton Square and in a conservation area. Chipperfield responded by excavating downwards to create hidden lower-ground levels, with only the upper three storeys visible from the exterior. There is also a sense of respectful discretion to the front elevation, with a recessed entrance and two integrated loggias arranged over the floors above, where a series of circular brick columns softens the rectangular outline of the villa.

The idea of an Italianate urban villa continues within, where the ground floor holds a generous entrance hall and other circulation spaces, including the main staircase to the piano nobile

above, where much of the floor is devoted to an open-plan living area, while the kitchen and breakfast room sit to the rear. The top storey consists largely of the extensive master suite.

Finishes and detailing are expertly crafted on every level of the concrete-framed building, from the handmade brickwork on the exterior to the travertine floors inside. Internally, natural tones and textures offer a soothing backdrop.

Chipperfield's philosophy places the resident at the centre of the design process. 'I think that the whole point of being an architect is to help raise the experience of everyday living,' he once said. 'It takes a lot of patience, a lot of experience, and a lot of unfashionable thought.'[25]

Left The idea of a contemporary piano nobile gives the main sitting room an elevated position, with framed views of the treetops in the adjoining square; this raised position also helps to ensure privacy, as well as a wealth of light.

Below The kitchen and breakfast room is to the rear of the house, behind the sitting room, yet still enjoys natural light and views over the sunken rear courtyard.

Above The principal bedrooms and bathrooms are generous in size and beautifully detailed, with elements such as the bath assuming a sculptural quality in this open space.

Opposite The creation of lower-ground and basement levels allowed for the provision of additional guest bedrooms and multiple amenities, including a swimming pool and sauna.

ASTLEY CASTLE
NUNEATON, WARWICKSHIRE
Witherford Watson Mann (2012)

Opposite A new residence has been created within the remaining shell of the original castle but with minimal disturbance to the outward character of the listed building.

Above The formerly derelict castle has been stabilized and resupported as part of the project to give the building a fresh life as a twenty-first-century rental retreat.

The revival of Astley Castle represents an extraordinary balancing act. The project, by architects Witherford Watson Mann, needed to respect the history of a ruined and listed building while creating a home for the present and, in doing so, ensuring Astley's future. Importantly, neither the architects nor their clients, the Landmark Trust, describe their work at Astley Castle in Warwickshire as a process of 'restoration' but rather as something more complex and ambiguous. 'If restoration implies a form of completion, a return to past wholeness, we have left the castle incomplete,' architect, practice co-founder and director William Mann (b. 1966) has written. 'In short, we have avoided completing or domesticating the remains, leaving the house at Astley open-ended and somewhat unsettling.'[26]

The history of the castle dates back to the Saxon era. The Astley family moated and crenellated the manor house during the thirteenth century and the site has been owned by three English queens, including Lady Jane Grey. During the 1950s Astley was turned into a hotel but was then badly damaged by a fire

in 1978. Over subsequent decades the ruined building deteriorated even further, despite being listed as an important and endangered heritage site. The Landmark Trust eventually decided to step in to try and save what remained of Astley Castle.

The Trust has a long-established track record of rescuing historic buildings by converting them into holiday lets, ensuring continued use and upkeep, along with countless pleasures for the many visitors who spend time at the properties. However, given the grave condition of Astley, where the roof had long gone and some of the walls had collapsed, an imaginative solution for the reinvention of the building was required. Witherford Watson Mann won a subsequent architectural competition with a plan that essentially inserted a new home within the remnants of the old.

'Much of the appeal of this project for us has been in the rigour and suppleness forced on us by the primary importance of caring for the artefact, the remains of the castle,' says Mann. 'From the beginning, our way of working has been discursive, moving between

Above and opposite The project consisted of a series of interventions within the outline of the historic building rather than a restoration programme, including the insertion of a new two-storey residence in one corner and a connecting staircase, while the castle's former reception rooms have been adapted into a spacious entrance hallway and multipurpose space topped by a skylight but with the outer windows remaining open to the elements.

the deep structure of the building and the way the whole is experienced, and between the logic of interventions and the cultural ripples these might generate.'[27]

The practice mapped the ruins and the surrounding grounds in great detail, as well as researching Astley's history in full. They were helped in some respects by the Trust's brief, which was for holiday accommodation that would take up only a third of the outline of the building without the need for some of the 'conventional expectations of both comfort and privacy' that one might expect in a permanent family home.

Having first stabilized the ruins, the architects decided to use the former reception rooms as a double-height entrance hallway, with an open communal space alongside it topped by a vast skylight. These areas serve as a hinterland between the exteriors and the interiors of a 'new' two-storey home that occupies one corner of the original Astley Castle. The bedrooms and bathrooms are on the ground floor while a new staircase leads up to a spacious, open-plan living area on the upper level. This piano nobile benefits from windows and walls of glass that look through the outer walls and broken apertures of the surrounding ruins to the parkland beyond.

The material palette for the new interventions is purposefully restrained. The architects opted for Danish brick, timber floors and ceilings,

Opposite The dining area on the upper level of the new dwelling looks over the hallway below. The new fenestration also looks through the original outer windows of the castle shell to frame glimpses of the landscape beyond.

Below Modern amenities and services have been carefully woven into the new residence, with careful attention given to the choice of materials and the way that they relate to the remaining fabric of the castle in terms of tone, texture and character.

wooden window frames and Spanish floor tiles, with the textures and tones sitting gently next to the fragments of the old castle. Fixtures, fittings and furniture mix the old and the new, but all within a carefully considered equation balancing function, comfort and simplicity. The resulting twenty-first-century retreat, set within the context of centuries of history, won the Stirling Prize for architecture in 2013.

'Preserving the emotional charge of the rich, uninterrupted life of this house was our goal,' concludes Mann. 'There may be grander or more vertiginous ruins, but there can be none as immediate or personal as the ruin that is simultaneously a house.'[28]

GRILLAGH WATER HOUSE

MAGHERA, COUNTY LONDONDERRY

Patrick Bradley (2014)

Opposite The upper storey of the house holds the main living spaces and an integrated balcony, which is within the cantilevered section to one side of the building; the Cor-ten-clad lower level is devoted to the private realm of bedrooms and bathrooms.

Above The house and the nearby studio forge a direct link with the landscape and the surroundings, sitting among the meadows of the family farm.

Patrick Bradley (b. 1980) describes himself as an architect and farmer. His two passions and preoccupations combine on the family farm near Maghera, where Bradley has created a unique home overlooking a mesmerizing landscape and an office for his practice alongside it. At the same time, his family continues to work the 65-acre farmstead that had been bought by Bradley's grandfather. Bradley explains that the farm is in his family's DNA and that although he enjoys travelling, when he returns he breathes 'a sigh of relief and happiness. You come back here and you are in the middle of the farm, the trees, the livestock. It's an oasis in my life.'

Having grown up on the farm, Bradley went to study architecture at Queen's University, Belfast. There were job offers in London and elsewhere, but Bradley felt that he needed to stay close to home, eventually taking a position with Northern Irish practice McGurk Architects. Having gained valuable experience of working on a wide range of scales and typologies, Bradley decided to set up his own firm, concentrating primarily on residential commissions. Soon after, he decided to build a house, identifying

the perfect spot a short walk from his parents' home and the outbuildings that stand around it. He expands:

> Every architect has a dream of building their own home. When you have a farm of this size you do know every step and every kind of atmosphere, so there are a couple of nice spots. But it's the same as when you are designing a house for a client: there's a puff of air saying this is the spot. I was down here thinking I've got the views, access to the farm, access to the road, but with this land around me, and it could work so well. It just felt right. After that, you let the ideas evolve rather than pushing something. But you also get more freedom when you work in rural areas like this and the flexibility to absorb the site so that you really understand it. Then the design process starts.

Bradley certainly chose his location well. The house looks over cattle pasture yet also sits close to the winding Grillagh River, which has

Above The sitting room forms part of the open-plan living area on the upper level, which connects with the elevated balcony and an adjoining roof terrace.

Opposite The kitchen and dining zone comprises part of the family living area on the upper level, which also holds the main entrance, accessed via a farm track positioned on higher ground than the surrounding meadows. The staircase leads to the lower floor where the family bathroom and bedrooms are located.

helped to gently shape the topography of the area. The new building rests at a point where the land dips down a notch, with the architect taking the decision to arrange the building over two floors to make best use of the shift in ground level.

After sketching out initial plans for the building, particularly its orientation and the way internal spaces would relate to the views, Bradley was drawn to the idea of using repurposed shipping containers to provide modular, semi-structural building blocks. Two 13.7m-long containers comprise the base of the house, with another pair placed at right angles on top of them, cantilevering outwards at one

end to meet the rising hillside and then floating over open space at the opposite end, where Bradley added an elevated balcony.

Bedrooms and bathrooms are on the lower-ground floor, the exterior of which Bradley coated in Cor-ten steel, a material that forms a natural outer layer of earthy rust that ties the house back to the land. The upper storey hosts the entrance and the largely open-plan living space, featuring a kitchen at one end, a dining area towards the centre and the lounge, which connects with the floating balcony and a roof terrace alongside (with an outdoor fireplace). Bradley says:

Below The design studio was added later and is just along the farm track from the house; it was also constructed using a shipping container with the two ends filled with glass, framing views over the rural landscape.

Opposite Seen from the cattle meadow, the cross-stacking of the containers and the two levels of the house become clear, as does the way that they work with the shifting topography.

When I started thinking about using the containers, I realized it wouldn't really affect the design I had in mind. I had already earmarked everything in terms of looking at the cows and the sun, as well as the orientation and the freedom of the outdoor spaces, so that never changed. But when I brought in the containers, it added another dimension of sculpting and crafting. But it was also about taking the simple idea of an agricultural shed and exaggerating it, so that's what I have done with the Cor-ten and then the grey cladding on top that blends with the sky. That's the idea: splitting the house into two forms and using two different types of material.

While initially basing his architectural practice in the house itself, Bradley later realized that he needed a dedicated workspace after getting married and starting a young family. Selecting a position between the new house and the farmhouse, he repurposed one more container as an office, painting the outside a soft golden colour, while a wall of glass at one end frames a view of Carn Mountain in the far distance. For Bradley, this short walk from home to office now offers an idyllic commute.

A HOUSE FOR ESSEX

WRABNESS, ESSEX

Grayson Perry and FAT Architecture (2014)

Opposite The house fuses multiple references and points of inspiration, ranging from pilgrimage shrines and follies to fairy-tale cottages, but also serves as a sophisticated twenty-first-century holiday retreat.

Above While the house is a distinct and original mix of art and architecture, it is also a gentle presence in the landscape, with the green ceramic tiles on the exterior and its corn-coloured roof helping to tie the building to its surroundings.

A House for Essex has become, much as intended, a place of pilgrimage. It draws those with a love of the Essex countryside, visitors with a passion for architecture and art lovers looking to experience the house in an immersive manner. As with all of the residences that form part of the Living Architecture collective, the house can be rented by visitors as a way of enjoying time in a twenty-first-century architect-designed home. But here, with the rounded results of a unique collaboration between FAT Architecture and artist Grayson Perry (b. 1960), there is an additional narrative layer explored in the crafted detailing and artworks threaded throughout the project, both inside and out.

'I would describe it as a very, very rare instance of a genuine collaboration between art and architecture,' says Charles Holland (b. 1969), FAT director and principal in charge of the build. 'A shared enthusiasm for decoration, ornament and the possibility of architecture as a storytelling art meant that we worked very closely and symbiotically.'

Coincidentally, both Holland and Perry grew up in Essex and went to school in nearby Chelmsford. Having been introduced by Alain de Botton (b. 1969), the founder of Living Architecture, the two found that they had many reference points in common and shared the pleasures of rediscovering a place that they know well. The semi-rural site is towards the northern edge of Essex, close to the River Stour, with Suffolk and the Shotley Peninsula on the other side of the water. There is a walking trail close by, as well as the ports of Harwich and Felixstowe, which all add to the sense of sitting in close proximity to an arterial route of sorts while reinforcing the idea of a modern interpretation of a pilgrimage chapel.

'The idea behind this project relates to buildings put up as memorials to loved ones, to follies, to eccentric home-built structures, to shrines, lighthouses and fairytales,' says artist, ceramicist, writer and presenter Grayson Perry. 'There are much-loved buildings all over the county and the country built in the same spirit.'

These various influences coalesced around Perry's invention of a fictional Essex resident, called Julie, whose story is told through the artist's ceramics and tapestries yet also

Opposite The interiors were designed around the narrative of the house's 'surrogate client', Julie, with repeated references to her life and times, yet there are also echoes of the Arts and Crafts movement in notions such as the 'great room', the inglenook fireplace and other integrated elements.

Above Layered with colour, pattern, textiles and art, the interiors also offer a processional movement through volume and space, with the entrance hall leading through to the stairway, then the kitchen/dining room (with bedrooms above) and finally the double-height living room, also known as the 'chapel', with its integrated seating and display niches.

referenced in the decorative tilework, detailing and other components. Julie became the guiding light for the evolution of the narrative of the house itself. Holland explains:

Julie acted as a sort of surrogate client, partly because, as a holiday home, the house doesn't have a client in the traditional sense. Julie's 'story' also allowed a conversation about taste and interiors in a way that is very rare in contemporary architecture. We would often ask ourselves questions such as 'what kind of kitchen would Julie have?' Or 'would she have an avocado bath suite?' At the same time, we were anxious to avoid the idea of the house as a stage set.

The site itself came with existing planning approval for a modern house to replace an early twentieth-century building that had once stood here. All agreed on the special character of the setting and of the need for a completely fresh design, which not only spoke of Julie but was a shrine to art. Importantly, this is also a contextual home that sits gently in the landscape while referencing the Arts and Crafts tradition in particular, with nods to Lutyens (see p. 15) and Voysey (see p. 39) seen, for example, in the inglenook fireplace that forms a key focal point in the living room.

Holland and Perry adopted a staggered formation for the house, which lends it something of a gingerbread cottage outline, yet the colours of the copper-coated roof and

Below The combined kitchen and dining room is a more intimately scaled space located between the entrance hallway and the great room; the stairway in the hall leads to two bedrooms positioned directly above the kitchen.

Opposite The two bedrooms and bathroom upstairs are modestly scaled yet carefully conceived, offering views of the adjoining great room below and also framed glimpses of the open Essex landscape; the porch is at the opposite end of the house to the main entrance.

emerald exterior tilework also help the building to blend into its surroundings. Internally, the layout offers a clear progression from the entrance to the hall and stairwell, followed by the kitchen/dining room and then the living room, or 'chapel', where representations of Julie occupy the niches and sacred places where you might – in another context – expect to see images of the saints. Upstairs, two modestly sized bedrooms sit above the kitchen, providing sleeping quarters for four at most, meaning that the house is generally enjoyed by small family groups or couples.

Colour, pattern and narrative can be seen everywhere in A House for Essex, with the interiors offering a text to be savoured over time.

Yet, as Holland suggests, the building itself is a gentle presence within the Essex countryside, rather like a folly floating in a meadow.

'I like the way that it sits in the landscape in a way that feels very right and strangely appropriate,' says Holland. 'It's obviously an eccentric object but the colours of the tiles relate to the fields and cowslips that surround it in summer and the roof matches the cornfields. So, in a funny way, it is contextual though not in an obvious manner. It's also very gratifying that people like staying there and it is unexpectedly homely and comfortable.'

FLINT HOUSE
WADDESDON ESTATE, BUCKINGHAMSHIRE
Skene Catling de la Peña (2015)

Opposite Among other things, the house explores the idea of emergence and stratification, with the flint-clad structure appearing to push upward from the ground like a geological feature in the landscape.

Above The project consists of two complementary structures on the same axis, namely the main residence and a smaller guest house; the relationship between the buildings adds to the dynamic character of the composition.

Gently emerging from a pastoral landscape, the Flint House has a unique geological quality. It sits among the open fields of the Waddesdon Estate, yet it also stands upon a subterranean ribbon of chalk and flint that makes its way from the South Downs all the way up to Norfolk. The house and annexe have the feeling of vivid topographical features pushing upwards from the ground, taking the form of ziggurats placed upon an axis and sitting opposite one another.

'When I first came to see the site it was the middle of winter, and I walked into the ploughed field alongside and by the time I was halfway my feet were covered in gigantic balls of clay,' recalls Charlotte Skene Catling (b. 1965), principal and co-founder at Skene Catling de la Peña. 'Then I looked down and saw that there was all this field flint around me in the soil. So my first response to the site really revolved around looking at the geology of it and discovering the extrusions of chalk and flint.'

Philanthropist Jacob Rothschild (b. 1936), who shares the guardianship of the nearby family seat of Waddeson Manor with the National Trust, commissioned the house.

The site itself was once home to a small, eighteenth-century farmstead but this had long since disappeared. It is also one of Lord Rothschild's favourite spots on the estate, with a small stream running through it.

'It was this little strip of land that had been worked around and farmed around,' says Skene Catling. 'But then on one side there were some trees, so the form emerged by taking the high point of those trees down to the centre of the site and playing with perspective.'

The master building became a stone wedge within the landscape, placed opposite a smaller guest house in a sculptural, mother-and-child arrangement. This stepped formation suggests a piece of land art as much as a work of architecture, reminiscent of, among other things, Adalberto Libera's Casa Malaparte on the island of Capri (1937). At the same time, the crafted quality of the Flint House is a vital element, with the stonework used to face the concrete-framed buildings forming stratas with subtle contrasts in tone and texture. These layers become lighter as they rise upwards, while the Norfolk- and Sussex-based artisans who worked

on the project also used various treatments of flint, both rounded and knapped. 'We go from huge pieces of black flint with gallets in the joints right up to the square blocks of chalk at the top,' Skene Catling says. 'There are these different levels ranging from dark to light so the building can fade into the sky visually.'

While the intrinsic character of the site is expressed in flint and stone, the way that the stream meets the land is also explored in the form of an integrated grotto tucked into one side of the house alongside the living room.

The main house, where the interiors were designed by David Mlinaric (b. 1939), has an ordered sequence of rooms and spaces over

Opposite and below The stonework used on the exterior of the two buildings is graded, with larger pieces of flint around the base and then a smaller, finer and knapped selection of stones further up, meaning that the tones of the coating become lighter as they rise towards the sky.

Below The dining room at the far end of the house includes a bespoke circular table made by the Flintman Company using fragments of chalk and flint.

Right Working in conjunction with the architecture of the house, interior design by David Mlinaric and the curated selection of artworks pick up on a number of key themes, including the importance of the pastoral in the English country-house tradition and the theme of the grotto, with Flint House's own grotto sitting just beyond the doors to the right.

three levels. The lowest part of the building holds the dining room, with its circular flint and chalk dining table, kitchen and library. The living room is almost at the heart of the plan, with a bridge overhead sitting between double-height zones, while also forming a mezzanine gallery connecting the main staircase to the bedrooms.

The master bedroom, at the highest point of the house, looks towards the rising hills. The combination of floor-to-ceiling glass and a balcony gives this tranquil space something of a treehouse feel, with an organic quality enhanced by the sage-green colour scheme and timber floors. A sense of calm pervades the entire house, as well as the more compact but self-contained guest house, with an ever-present sense of connection to the open landscape.

LIFE HOUSE
LLANBISTER, POWYS
John Pawson (2016)

The purpose of Living Architecture, founded by Alain de Botton (b. 1969), is to offer its guests the opportunity to experience the best in modern architecture and design for themselves. In the design of Life House, in a rural Welsh valley, de Botton and architect John Pawson (b. 1949) took the theme of 'experience' to a new level within an original sanctuary that is not only connected to its setting but also offers visitors a handful of carefully curated pleasures.

'From the beginning Alain and I talked in terms of the idea of a secular monastery, where guests could spend some time exploring different rules for living,' says Pawson. 'He wanted to create a retreat where people could come together or retreat into private space for a range of contemplative and social activities, from reading and taking a bath to gathering together to prepare and share meals. All this made perfect sense to me.'

Although Pawson has designed many houses, as well as a monastery, he welcomed the chance to work on a residential project that offered greater interaction with a wide spectrum of visitors over time. There was also the temptation

of the setting in the Welsh Marches with few neighbouring houses in sight. The overall feeling here is one of peacefulness and calm, which is very much in keeping with the ethos of Life House. As Pawson describes:

It was the wildness of the setting that made the greatest impression. You really feel that you have made a journey to get there and I think this is important to your subsequent experience of being in the house. It's not so much the time that it takes but the reality of heading out into this remote landscape. I loved the contrast between the intimacy of the folds and clefts of the site and the broad drama of the outlook. I wanted to make a house that was deeply comfortable to be in, but without isolating or insulating its inhabitants from everything that is special about being in so elemental a place.

As Pawson suggests, the journey continues within the house itself. Composed of 80,000 handmade Danish bricks, the single-storey

home is pushed gently into the slope of the hillside, with the grey-black coat of exterior brickwork intended to echo the gorse and darker tones of the surrounding hills. Stepping inside, the palette is much lighter, with the brick and light woodwork tying in with the paler grasses and vegetation. Two strong lines of circulation run through the L-shaped building, enhancing the 'promenade architecturale'. The first links the welcoming entrance hallway to the first of the bedroom suites to one side and then the communal living space on the other, including an open-plan kitchen, dining area and lounge. A second corridor then leads into the sloping gradient of the hill, passing two further bedroom suites before reaching a contemplation chamber that is partially immersed in the ground itself

Left The seating area is arranged around the corner window and the Tile Stove wood burner by Dick van Hoff (b. 1971); the sofa and coffee table are John Pawson designs.

Below The dining area and kitchen are at the other side of the open-plan living area, with a John Pawson-designed dining table complemented by dining chairs by Hans Wegner (1914–2007).

Above The bedrooms explore various kinds of experiences and pleasures, as seen in the room devoted to music, complete with audio equipment and a curated collection of compact discs.

Opposite Other experiential spaces in the house include the meditation room and a bedroom dedicated to the enjoyment of reading, featuring a library of books curated by Alain de Botton.

but looks upwards to a skylight that opens at the touch of a switch.

'As we engage with unfamiliar architectural spaces, we engage with ourselves,' de Botton and Alison Morris wrote in their guidebook to Life House. 'And while we do so, the most fundamental of everyday rituals…all become opportunities for recovering lost significance and pleasure.' The rituals chosen by de Botton and Pawson include social and more intimate experiences, such as talking, listening and cooking, with the guide offering a small number of recipes and possibilities, while a specially

commissioned artwork in the great room by Hamish Fulton (b. 1946) celebrates the activity of walking through the surrounding countryside.

Bedrooms are also designed around key rituals such as bathing, listening to music and reading; a hi-fi system comes with a variety of CDs chosen by Pawson's son, while de Botton has curated a selection of books in the reading suite. 'The idea was to choose ordinary, everyday activities and allow people to experience these immersively in a series of specifically tuned, sensuous environments so that they would become almost meditative acts,' says Pawson.

RUINS STUDIO
DUMFRIES, DUMFRIES AND GALLOWAY
Lily Jencks and Nathanael Dorent (2016)

Opposite Lily Jencks's family retreat sits within the ruins of a former farmstead, which is fully off-grid given the distance of the house from any mains services.

Above The new residence has been slotted into the stone outline of a former barn on a gently sloping hillside and enjoys open views of the surrounding landscape.

Sitting in a magical position on a Dumfriesshire hillside, the ruins of a nineteenth-century barn and adjoining farmhouse were part of Lily Jencks's childhood. The ruins are not far from the family estate, where Jencks (b. 1980) spent many of her holidays, and which is also the location of the Garden of Cosmic Speculation, designed by her late father Charles Jencks (see p. 157). The derelict farmstead was acquired many years ago by Lily 's mother, artist, writer and garden designer Maggie Keswick Jencks (1941–1995), who was captivated by the quiet beauty of the surroundings and the open vista across the Borders landscape.

'It was a place that we used to walk to from our family house and go and sit and just admire the view,' says Lily. 'My mother bought the land as a place to build an artist's studio, but she never got around to doing it. Every time we walked up, there was this idea we could have something here, because it is such a fantastic place to be where you can spend all your time watching the view like a television.'

It was only after Lily had set up her own architectural practice and got married that she started thinking about building a fresh family retreat on the site of the ruins. She concentrated initially on the ruined barn, which runs across the hillside and looks down into the valley. Collaborating with friend and fellow architect Nathanael Dorent (b. 1984), Jencks developed ideas for a layered building that would make use of the remnants of the stone walls. Within this she created a building within a building, using a steel-and-timber frame finished in a black coat of waterproof rubber, known as EPDM, punctuated by large windows and skylights. Internally, Jencks introduced a third layer using a curvaceous, internal tube made with a timber framework covered in glass-reinforced plastic. While the exteriors of the house are dark and somewhat enigmatic, the interiors are light, sculptural and fluid, with one space flowing gently into the next.

'The design was really a result of the logic that we applied to the barn, in that the windows would go where there were existing window openings in the stone walls and then the interior curving tube would fit within that, also accommodating these openings and the thickness of the walls,' states Jencks. 'We were

Opposite The light, free-flowing interior contrasts with the dark stonework and cladding on the exterior, with the main family living spaces situated in a fluid sequence at the centre of the building.

Above The ribbon window by the dining table gives a sense of the panoramic views out across the hills and valleys of Dumfries from this elevated position.

very lucky that the logic worked well but we also studied it a lot, building everything digitally on the computer and making lots of physical models, so there was time to review and finesse it.'

Another important consideration was the lack of standard services. Trying to bring cabled electricity up from the nearest road was unaffordable, so Jencks decided to go off-grid. The building is highly insulated, while the orientation and quality of natural light within the studio reduces the need for artificial lighting. Having taken this into account, Jencks then opted for a range of heat and energy solutions, including two wood-burning stoves and a photovoltaic array situated a short distance from

the house, complemented by battery storage; a back-up generator running on portable gas tanks can also be called upon. Jencks explains:

It is very satisfying to be off-grid. There's not one single solution but many different ways of making an off-the-grid lifestyle more attainable and enjoyable. We use very little electricity during the long summer evenings and hardly turn the lights on during the day, as the house is so light, and then in the winter we often use the fires and candles. Watching our electricity use and solar power can be quite addictive.

Below and opposite The remnants of the stone walls of the old barn serve as partial partitions between the key parts of the house, with bedrooms at either end of the building and the living spaces and main entrance in between. At the same time, the old apertures and openings in the stone walls define the new fenestration of Ruins Studio, adding to the sense of architectural layering and contrasts between old and new.

While the house provides a golden example of both off-the-grid living and imaginative, adaptive reuse in terms of recycling the ruins of the existing buildings – with potential ideas for the remains of the farmhouse also under consideration – this is also a much-loved family home, now shared with two young children.

'It is a great house for the kids,' says Jencks. 'There are two gentle ramps in the house, so of course they love sliding down them and turning their coats into sledges. It is pretty exposed here and if there's a storm it can be blustery, but when you shut the door it's silent and you can just watch the drama unfold outside. We feel very nested, safe and at home.'

GREENWAYS
COOMBE PARK, SURREY
Nick Eldridge (2017)

Opposite The mature oak in the rear garden became a focal point in the design of the house, with both the architectural composition and landscaping working around the tree, resulting in a trefoil plan that is replicated in the shape of the pool.

Above Curving lines and rounded forms are repeated in every part of the house, including the elevated bedroom pod that floats above the entrance lobby and the main living spaces arranged on the lower-ground floor.

With its curvaceous, sculptural form Greenways is quite unlike any of the neighbouring neo-classical mansions within this secluded and leafy enclave situated upon the southwestern edge of the capital. Yet, at the same time, this decidedly twenty-first-century home is one of the most discreet houses here, with much of the residence – designed by architect Nick Eldridge (b. 1957) and his practice – tucked away so that it connects with the spacious rear garden rather than the private roadway alongside.

In many ways, the Manser Medal-winning Greenways was a departure. It is one of the most adventurous buildings designed by Eldridge to date and is the product of a close collaboration between the architect and a client who wanted to create a truly unique home different to anything around it. However, the design was also highly contextual in the way that it responded to the gently sloping site and particularly the majestic oak tree that inhabits the rear garden.

'It is one of the most organic houses that we have designed and the form really came out of the site itself,' says Eldridge. 'The 100-year-old oak tree was the generator of the curved walls

because it seemed like a good focal point for the view from the main living space and helped to inspire the first curve that I set down on paper. Then we began to create repetitions of that arc and arrived at this trefoil shape.'

The trefoil became the defining element of the house, which replaced a 1950s bungalow, and helped to establish various key zones on the lower-ground floor. Eldridge gently pushed the lower level, comprising the living area, into the slope of the hill so that this space was invisible to the street but opened up via rounded walls of floor-to-ceiling glass to the adjoining terrace and garden. The sunken living area is arranged around a fireplace with a dramatic marble surround and flows through to the kitchen, and then a semi-separate study beyond. Another part of the trefoil holds a media room and bedroom, with all of the zones revolving around a central spiral staircase built around a concrete column that supports the building. Eldridge explains:

The core of the staircase is an important structural element as it's effectively one of the two columns that help to support

Opposite The spiral staircase holds two routes, with the outer treads leading down to the main reception area at garden level while an inner, secret stairway leads upwards to the master bedroom at the top of the house.

Below The sunken seating area on the lower-ground floor contains bespoke sofas arranged around the views and the feature fireplace, with its brass detailing and marble surround.

the floating master suite that we designed at the top of the house. On the outside of the core the stairs lead down to the main living space from the entrance hallway, which is really all there is at ground-floor level. Inside the core there is a secondary, private stairway that allows you to walk right up from the living space at lower ground to the master suite on the first floor without being seen from the road, so it really enhances the sense of privacy. The most radical element of the design, apart from the shape, was that there is effectively no ground floor as you see the house from the street but only a void that you can see right through. It really is a hidden house.

The sinuous outline of the top storey, consisting of the master bedroom suite, was coated in a privacy screen made from anodized aluminium tubes with a trefoil profile. This rounded brise soleil enhances the sculptural quality of the building, while adding another textural layer to the dynamic composition.

Another critical aspect of the project was a commitment, shared by both architect and client, to choose materials of quality and character throughout. The house is made with a concrete framework and expanses of glass, but Eldridge also wanted to make extensive use of natural materials for the internal finishes, including the suspended oak staircase, hung on brass rods, and the engineered oak floors.

The kitchen is a bespoke design, as is the fitted desk in the study, while marble was used in the bathrooms and for the feature fire surround in the seating area. Eldridge explains:

We were led by the client's interest in more luxurious materials, like brass and marble. We decided to go to the Carrara quarry in Italy and buy a 20-ton block that was then cut and book matched as far as possible, so we had the continuity on the walls and floors of the bathroom and the same for the fireplace. The triumph of those kind of exercises was that by going direct to the source you can get bespoke elements made for the price of off-the-shelf elements.

The level of craftsmanship and detailing throughout the house is superlative. Outside, the gardens were carefully landscaped while preserving the oak tree and other mature planting, and a naturally filtered swimming pond was introduced. In the shape of the pool, Eldridge opted once again to repeat the trefoil that brings the house to life. 'We submitted a model of the building to the Royal Academy for the Summer Exhibition and they actually exhibited it in the sculpture gallery rather than the space for architecture,' says Eldridge. 'It raises this question about where the divide between architecture and art might be and for us, as architects, we hope that architecture can be art.'

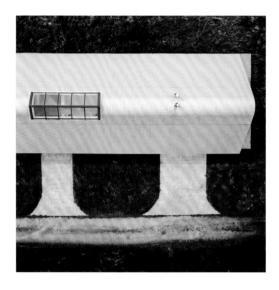

BRIONGOS MACKINNON HOUSE

STRATHAVEN AIRFIELD, SOUTH LANARKSHIRE

Richard Murphy (2019)

Opposite The house enjoys open views across the airfield from its upper levels, making it a unique monitoring station for daily air traffic as well as an original home.

Above The new building references the neighbouring hangars on the airfield in its form and use of materials yet is also a distinctly modern composition, with a rounded roofline and other curvaceous elements that soften the house and lend it a sculptural quality.

A shared passion for flying helped to forge a perfect understanding between an architect and his clients when it came to the challenge of building a contemporary home on the open grounds of a Scottish airfield. Strathaven Airfield sits upon a plateau in open countryside to the south of Glasgow and East Kilbride and, at nearly 259 m (850 feet) above sea level, is one of the highest working aerodromes in the region. The setting is sublime yet the altitude means that the weather can be extreme and the winters are often harsh. Any new building needs to be able to withstand these conditions, and the Briongos MacKinnon House is rugged and hard wearing, but also sculptural, original and highly imaginative.

The house was designed by Edinburgh-based architect Richard Murphy (b. 1955) for journalist-turned-flying-instructor Colin MacKinnnon and his partner, trapeze artist Marta Briongos. The couple were living in Glasgow when they first spotted the airfield on aerial trips, with MacKinnon then following up with initial enquiries about the site. 'I used to come to the airfield occasionally from Cumbernauld and

I could see that it was almost derelict,' says MacKinnon. 'There was an old hangar that was being propped up and the airfield was being used as a gliding club. But the last time they were based here, the club used it for nine hours in a whole year. People hardly even knew that there was an airfield here.'

Soon after, the site was put up for sale and the couple's bid was accepted. One of their earliest projects was a new hangar, but Briongos and MacKinnon soon started thinking about building a home here that would allow them to live in situ while managing the revived airfield. Sharing an interest in contemporary architecture, the couple decided to approach Richard Murphy about the project. Murphy explains:

The clients knew about the practice from some publicity that we had received from other domestic projects in Scotland and it was a happy coincidence that we were both microlight pilots. Of course, I was fascinated by a project that I could fly into. The site is not for the agoraphobic,

in that it's an area of upland farming with
large fields, some forestry and distant
views of one of Europe's biggest on-shore
windfarms. Near to hand there were
the hangars and an old Nissen hut, but
otherwise there's a lot of open space and
grass. But, for me, the site was highly
unusual because we are used to squeezing
houses into little gap sites in Edinburgh
and dealing with all the issues of working
in a conservation area. Here, the absence
of constraints and the open landscape was,
to begin with, bewildering.

Murphy and his clients convinced the local
planners that they should be allowed to erect a
new house at Strathaven based on the precedent
of working farmhouses built in agricultural
settings. As with a farmstead, MacKinnon
and Briongos are – in a sense – working the
land while looking after their surroundings.
And the design of the house itself takes
inspiration from the countryside context as
well as the curvaceous, corrugated-metal coating
of the Nissen hut. Other points of reference
include the work of Australian master architect
Glenn Murcutt (b. 1936), particularly his Marie
Short House in rural New South Wales (1975),
and his idea of 'touching the earth lightly'.

Sitting on the edge of the airstrip, the
new steel-framed house is clad in corrugated
aluminium, including the rounded roofline.
Service spaces and guest bedrooms are all
located on the ground floor, while the piano

Below The design of the house enables constant connections with not only the airfield but also the open landscape beyond it, with the building engaging with the countryside over the changing seasons and shifting weather patterns.

Opposite The mezzanine studio and study at the top of the house gives views in two directions, meaning that the owners can keep an eye on the airfield as they work; the central skylight offers another valuable source of natural light as well as an oculus upon the open sky.

nobile holding the main living spaces looks over the open airfield and the landscape beyond. The master suite also sits at one end of this principal level, while a mezzanine gallery floating above the semi-open-plan kitchen, dining area and seating zone serves as a home office/studio, offering a bird's-eye view of the aerial traffic.

The house was designed to be as hard wearing and as thermally efficient as possible, reducing its energy needs. These are largely met by a biomass boiler on the ground floor, fed by wood pellets from an adjoining store room, while warming up the underfloor heating. The new house met all of MacKinnon and Briongos's requirements and then managed to exceed them.

'We really fell in love with the plans and sketches that Richard did for us,' confirms Briongos. 'The curves of the house make it very sensual and give the house a real softness. For us, that makes it much more beautiful than a house full of angles and edges.'

NITHURST FARM

SOUTH DOWNS NATIONAL PARK, WEST SUSSEX
Adam Richards (2019)

Opposite On the site of a former farmstead, surrounded by pasture and woodland, the new house enjoys a sense of peaceful isolation within the landscape.

Above The bucolic setting, without a neighbour in sight, allows the key qualities of the house to be appreciated more fully, particularly its original form, the choice of materials and its highly crafted character.

There is something of a fairy-tale quality to the house that architect Adam Richards (b. 1967) has designed and built for himself and his family in the Sussex countryside. It is partly to do with the idyllic setting, with the house hidden away in a green bowl in the landscape, with mature trees all around and a pasture populated by grazing sheep immediately in front of it. But there are also the multiple layers of stories and references that have fed into the narrative of the house, including the inspiration provided by English follies floating in bucolic surroundings.

'Two of the closest buildings to the house are actually folly towers, so that allowed us to build on this idea that follies are part of the local scene and construct a narrative for the planners,' says Richards, who also designed the Ditchling Museum of Art + Craft in Sussex (2013). 'But quite a few people have said that it looks like something in Tuscany and there is this sense of the house rising up to meet the slope of the hill and reflecting the shape of the landscape.'

Although mostly based in London for many years, Richards and his wife Jessica, who is a teacher, found themselves spending more and more time in Sussex. Eventually they bought a small farmer's cottage there, mostly for weekends and holidays, but with the arrival of three young children the pressure began to grow for more living space, while the attractions of Sussex increasingly seemed to outweigh those of Shoreditch. Richards began working on ideas for a new country house and found that the local planners embraced the proposal to replace their cottage with something more substantial and ambitious.

'The cottage was not a pretty thing and the barns alongside it, which we have kept, were actually much more attractive', continues Richards. 'We wanted the house to sit well with the barns, as we really like them both, and we wanted the grain of the materials that we used in the house to complement them without aping them.'

Richards designed a three-storey building that ascends like a ziggurat as it reaches the master bedroom suite on the top floor, which is crowned with a tall chimney. The house is concrete-framed but coated in crafted brickwork, with the majority of the windows framed by

Below The concrete units around the kitchen and dining area serve a structural purpose yet also hold amenities and utilities, including a pantry and cloakroom; at the same time, they help to define various zones around them.

Right The sitting room, or solar, marks the final destination in a thoughtful architectural journey that carries you to the house and through it, representing a process of homecoming enriched by multiple themes and references. The tapestries are seventeenth- and eighteenth-century pieces, while the collection of artworks floating on the tapestries is by Robert Mangold (b. 1937).

characterful arches while the tiered roofline is coated in black zinc.

Stepping into the house, the thoughtful 'promenade architecturale' begins with a spacious, double-height family room: a twenty-first-century equivalent of the 'great room', with space enough for a kitchen, dining area and a family room. A series of structural concrete towers to either side of this family-friendly living area holds service spaces, including a pantry, cloakroom and laundry.

Beyond the great room, a doorway leads through to a more enclosed circulation zone that holds not only the stairway but also a winding corridor leading through to the light-filled sitting room, or 'solar'. With picture windows, looking out onto the landscape and the woods, this is a space full of light and drama, enhanced by the sequence of tapestries and

Opposite Contrasts in materials and textures are evident throughout the interiors, with the raw concrete juxtaposed with the brick arches around the windows and organic elements such as the wooden floors and natural fibre carpets.

Below The bedrooms, including the twin sleeping spaces at the summit of the house, enjoy views over the treetops, while the master bathroom on the uppermost level is a welcoming, restful space floating above the surrounding landscape.

artworks on the walls. One of the key points of inspiration here was the film *Stalker* (1979), directed by Andrei Tarkovsky, which follows a long, slow journey to a mystical room.

'I'm a bit obsessed with that film and this idea of a journey to a room where your wishes come true,' Richards says. 'It translated into wanting to design the most beautiful space that I possibly could and, in a way, building a house for yourself and your family is all about finding a home in the world, so that's what this room represented for me. It's a special space, but also the end of the journey.'

Upstairs, the bedrooms for the children and guests are positioned at mid-level. Then, heading up a narrow secondary staircase, Richards created a fully bespoke suite for

himself and his wife to deal with his tendency towards snoring. The master bedroom is neatly split into two halves, with the twin spaces lightly separated by the position of the stairway, yet they both link easily with each other and with a spacious, shared bathroom on the same level.

'It's all connected together by this circular route and there are these fantastic views,' enthuses Richards. 'There's this wonderful feeling that you are right at the top of the house, looking out. We have this sense of waking up with a mini baptism every day.'

HANNINGTON FARM

HOLCOT, NORTHAMPTONSHIRE

James Gorst (2019)

There is a true sense of discovery built into the moment of arrival at Hannington Farm. A long driveway carries you past the fields and farm buildings until you dip down and turn a corner, just as the farmhouse gradually reveals itself within the landscape. Similarly, the composition of the house draws you naturally towards the front door, which is set in the fold between two wings of the Y-shaped building. Yet, beyond this carefully conceived 'promenade architecturale', perhaps the most striking impression within the house itself is one of tranquillity and calm.

'It was about delaying that moment when you first see the house so you that can really appreciate the view and begin to understand why the house is here,' says architect James Gorst (b. 1950). 'It's building this feeling of expectation as you pass these black timber buildings, such as the farm manager's cottage and the stables. Then you arrive at the entrance, which is relatively enclosed. But once you are inside, then you finally see the garden, the lake and the landscape. Everything is revealed.'

The farmhouse sits within a 300-acre working deer farm, run on organic farming principles. Here, Gorst was asked to design a new family home, as well as the complementary working barns and sheds, on the site of a series of derelict agricultural buildings. Given the sensitivity of the setting and the natural beauty of the surroundings, Gorst applied for permission to build Hannington Farm under the 'country house clause' of the national planning framework, which allows for one-off, innovative rural homes only if they are of exceptional architectural quality and where the immediate setting would be enhanced by the project. Such was the case with Hannington, where the house is both characterful and contextual, but also forms part of a wider programme of landscape restoration and revival.

While the house itself is clearly contemporary in its design, the composition was informed by the farmstead tradition, as well as the history of grander English country estates. There are vernacular references throughout, and the use of natural materials – the Cotswolds stonework used to clad the timber-framed building and the rugged slate shingles for the roof – creates a pleasing sense of unity and cohesion.

Opposite The structural laminated beams in the sitting room enrich the character of the space, while the sense of height, light and volume adds to the feeling of open welcome; the main dining area sits at the other end of this space.

Below The kitchen and breakfast room enjoys views over the gardens and grounds to the farmland beyond, as well as connections to the terrace.

Nonetheless, the first ideas about composition and form were inspired by the natural surroundings. Gorst explains:

The contours of the land helped to generate the early ideas for the scheme. We decided to create two artificial lakes below the house, which also received all the rainwater from the buildings. All of the pitched roofs are asymmetrical and it looks reassuring in the landscape, but it's also about taking the vernacular and giving it a twist. The tall chimneys are

almost like Italian campaniles and we were very pleased with those; it's almost like a touch of San Gimignano in the Northamptonshire countryside.

The pinwheel formation of the house, with its three distinct wings revolving around the central hallway and staircase, is well suited to modern family life. The main wing holds a double-height living/dining room as well as a kitchen, while the master suite is situated upstairs within this part of the house. Of the other two parts of the pinwheel, one is devoted to leisure spaces at

ground level with children's bedrooms above, while the third spoke hosts a double-height indoor pool and ancillary spaces, including a combined wine cellar and charcuterie.

'The clients were really passionate about creating a unique place for their children to grow up in,' says Gorst. 'They were keen to create a family home that would be there for the duration, so we wanted to carry the design process through every detail and ensure a seamless connection between the architecture and the interiors.'

The cross-laminated timber beams that form part of the structural framework of the house are largely left exposed and fully expressed, adding to the intrinsic character of the house. The focus on craftsmanship,

organic material and fine detailing continues throughout the home, including the bespoke staircase, while shifts in height and volume add a more dynamic element. Another vital ingredient is the indoor–outdoor relationship, explored via framed views of the water garden to one side of the house and, of course, the open vista to the other.

'The house continues to delight and enthral us,' confirm Gorst's clients. 'The house is an extraordinary piece of architecture and delivers on the sustainable credentials that were so important to us. And the plan is wonderfully considered with the different wings that allow our family life to play out while discreetly catering to young children, adults and guests along with all of the paraphernalia of family life.'

SARTFELL RESTORATIVE RURAL RETREAT

ISLE OF MAN

Foster Lomas (2019)

Opposite In an elevated position on the mountainside, the new retreat is next to a period cottage known as Cloud Nine. The interlinked elements benefit from views across the landscape and towards the coast.

Above The stonework used to coat the new building anchors the house to the site, while referencing traditional Manx cottages and the technique of dry-stone walls common to the island.

Just three days into their first visit to the Isle of Man, Peter and Carole Lillywhite became the owners of a cottage on the slopes of Sartfell mountain. Known as Cloud Nine, the traditional nineteenth-century cottage came with $7\frac{1}{2}$ acres of farmland along with open views across the surrounding landscape. The Lillywhites decided to realize a long-held dream to create a nature reserve, as well as an extraordinary new home for themselves, which became the first house on the island to win national and regional awards from RIBA, while also being shortlisted for its House of the Year prize. Peter, who had been living in Sydney with his wife, elaborates:

We loved the Isle of Man immediately because of its natural beauty. The famous English botanist David Bellamy once said that the island is a microcosm of the British Isles, with parts like Scotland, Wales, Ireland and England. To cut a long story short, over the next three years we got permission to build a new house, which is technically an extension to the existing cottage, which could be used

as a rental for eco tourists and any other visitors interested in all that the Isle of Man has to offer. More importantly, we were given permission to turn the land into a nature reserve, which became even more acceptable after the island got UNESCO Biosphere status.

The Sartfell Restorative Rural Retreat became a joint project for Peter, a scientist, academic and consultant, and his wife Carole, who has a background in education. They contacted architects Foster Lomas, who began with a 'forensic' study of the site and setting, including its history, weather patterns and ecology, with the Manx Wildlife Trust engaged to investigate the existing flora. This research became the basis for a proposal that would see a new building constructed alongside the old, with a low-lying link tying the two structures together while preserving the independent character of each. Architect William Foster (b. 1974) explains:

We had to make sure that the existing Cloud Nine cottage could still be enjoyed

297

Opposite Ribbons of glass frame key views across the island landscape, with the house serving as an observatory for appreciating the natural habitat and, in particular, the birdlife.

Above The design of the house balances sensitivity to its surroundings with the desire to constantly engage with its setting, seen in all parts of the building, including relatively functional spaces such as the kitchen.

by the islanders as they drove over the mountain road. So we decided to submerge the new building to reduce its visual impact. The local ruined Manx cottages, known as 'tholtans', and the large number of dry-stone walls weaved around the site made an immediate impression on our approach to the design and we also wanted our building to be inhabited by nature, with sheltered habitats for flora and fauna. We realized that we could harvest stone and soil from the site that would create these opportunities.

Excavating stone to help construct and clad the new addition allowed for the creation of a new lake, which formed a fresh habitat in itself, while the use of stonework to wrap the new eco bunker anchored the building to the site and made it dissolve into the mountain. The largely two-storey residence was pushed into the hillside, using a concrete structure mitigated by a range of eco-sensitive solutions that have given the building a zero-carbon level of performance and the ability to function off-grid, an ambition shared by the architects and their clients. These solutions involved high-specification insulation and triple glazing, green roofs, an on-site water source and a mechanical ventilation and heat-recovery system (MVHR), as well as green energy production from a lake-source heat pump.

Bedrooms are positioned at lower-ground level, with the main living spaces above and benefiting from ribbon and picture windows

facing the open landscape in the manner of a sophisticated observatory. A triple-height staircase leads to a study and viewing post right at the top of the building. It also doubles as a knowledge centre, with stacked bookcases comprising a substantial library at the heart of the building. The open views from the house carry across the fields towards the coast and the Irish Sea. The surrounding farmland has been fully restored and resuscitated to create a dedicated nature reserve, while plans for a modest visitors' centre are underway.

'We have already had successes with turning the farmland back to nature,' says Dr Lillywhite, a zoologist and neurobiologist. 'As an indicator of how our wild native plants have flourished, we found one orchid in year one and we now have over a thousand native Isle of Man orchids. We have hen harriers, buzzards, kestrels, peregrine falcons, siskin, finches, wheatears, redstarts, buntings and so on, so we also designed the house to be a stunning bird-hide.'

Above Although the design of the house responds to the open vista, elements such as the fireplace and staircase also offer focal points, with the stairwell serving as a library or knowledge centre as well.

Opposite The framing of key views is a vital ingredient of the design of the interior, as seen in the living room where the views stretch as far as the Irish Sea.

SECULAR RETREAT
CHIVELSTONE, SOUTH DEVON
Peter Zumthor (2019)

Surrounded by a ring of mature Monterey pines, framing views of the Devon landscape beyond, the Secular Retreat has something of a dream-like quality to it. Perched on a quiet hilltop, the house is a place 'dedicated to calm, reflection and perspective', yet this is also a kind of observatory for communing with nature, history and geography within a unique part of England. Excluding his temporary Serpentine Pavilion of 2011, it is also the only completed British project by esteemed Swiss architect Peter Zumthor (b. 1943). Best known for his imaginative responses to dramatic landscapes and his commitment to artisanal craftsmanship, as seen in his famous Thermal Baths at Vals (1996), Zumthor translates these themes to a West Country context.

'I love beautiful landscapes,' says the Pritzker Prize-winning architect. 'I fell in love straight away with the hillside, the rolling hills, the views, the ring of wonderful pines. It was a privilege to think about a house in this setting. Landscape and architecture fused within the design to the highest extent.'

Secular Retreat can be seen as the first and last holiday retreat within de Botton's Living Architecture programme, established with the aim of allowing you to experience great modern architecture at first hand. Running over ten years in all, the highly ambitious Secular Retreat was a complex and sometimes challenging project that tested the commitment of all concerned yet resulted in a masterpiece.

'I produce originals,' states Zumthor. 'I react to sites and programmes, so my buildings all look different. Once they are there, I love them all; it's like having children. In terms of architecture, the house in Chivelstone might be my contribution to the old typology of the villa in the countryside.'

The hilltop was formerly occupied by a timber-framed kit house imported during the 1950s by the local landowner, who also planted the trees around the building. Past its useful life and unsuited to the seasonal extremes in this exposed location, the house was ready for replacement and the mesmerizing site was seen by de Botton and Living Architecture director Mark Robinson as a golden opportunity to create something very special. Zumthor was, eventually, persuaded to accept the commission.

Opposite The house rests on a Devon hilltop, the site of a former farmhouse, with views of the countryside all around.

Above A ring of mature Monterey pines runs around the house, on the one hand helping to protect and encircle the retreat, on the other offering views of the surrounding landscape through the trees.

The initial design took inspiration from the tors and standing stones of the region, but proved too large and too challenging to build, consisting as it did of a series of interconnected pavilions with stone supports. The revised and completed design offers an enjoyable balance between an open and engaging communal space, topped by a high cantilevered roof canopy held aloft by monolithic slabs of rammed and stratified concrete, and two bedroom wings holding a total of five suites. Each suite pushes out into the landscape and enjoys a unique and private vista of its own.

Construction took five years, with the stone floors alone taking a year to complete. Zumthor was asked to work on every aspect of the design, including the lighting, fitted furniture and the loose furniture, such as the dining table,

Left The bands of cast concrete used to create the house suggest geological strata emerging from an ancient site, while the rooftop canopy is reminiscent of a megalith laid over a barrow by way of protection.

Below The kitchen and dining area leads out to a terrace on one side of the building, which drops down gently to the gardens around the house within the ring of pines.

Below The bespoke kitchen includes a monolithic bank of units that demarcates the entrance hallway on the opposite side.

Right Furniture and lighting by Peter Zumthor grace the seating area, arranged around the fireplace, and the dining area alongside, with the exception of the dining chairs that were designed by Swiss architect Max Ernst Haefeli (1901–1976) during the 1920s.

armchairs, sofas and side tables in the living area, which features high walls of floor-to-ceiling glass drawing in the natural surroundings, which seem to become a part of the house itself.

'Once the design evolved and began to set itself into the landscape in my mind, to think of the building as a secular retreat came to me in a natural way,' expands Zumthor. 'A group of people meets in a big space and then retreats to their personal room whenever they want. It's a house of dignity, simplicity.'

While the site was found in 2007, Secular Retreat was only opened to guests in 2019. The commitment to detail is evident throughout a house that has been described as Zumthor's 'Gesamtkunstwerk', or total work of art.

MOLE HOUSE
HACKNEY, LONDON
David Adjaye and Sue Webster (2019)

Opposite The verdant planting in the front garden contrasts with the textured walls of the house and the brickwork of the boundaries, while the sky and trees are reflected in the mirrored coating placed over the windows of the living area of the piano nobile.

Above Mole House sits on a triangular wedge of land formed by the convergence of two streets; this arrangement creates a distinctive framework and setting for the house that enhances its sculptural quality.

David Adjaye (b. 1966) has always collaborated closely with artists, painters and sculptors. The resulting houses, particularly in London, challenge conventional stereotypes of domesticity. Such experimental projects, from Elektra House (2000) onwards, often involve spaces for the display or making of art, as well as stretching definitions of the domestic realm.

Artist Sue Webster (b. 1967) has worked with Adjaye on not just one but two occasions. In 2002, Webster and her then partner and fellow artist Tim Noble (b. 1966) completed the Dirty House & Studio, which comprised the radical reinvention of a former factory in Shoreditch. Ten years later, in 2012, Webster began working with Adjaye on a second project, known as the Mole House. Webster says:

The Dirty House was radical and iconic. But I didn't want to do the same thing again…and this building, originally two Victorian houses, came with this amazing history of the Mole Man. The whole thing was a complete and utter mess and my builder said it would be cheaper to knock it down and rebuild it. But that made no sense to me. I wanted to keep the façade as it was and then rebuild it on the inside.[29]

The Mole Man's real name was William Lyttle (1931–2010). He earned his moniker on account of the extensive excavations that he made to his home, tunnelling down into his cellars and beyond, as well as out into the garden. The local council became concerned that he had excavated out under the two neighbouring pavements and roads on either side of the house and rerouted the local bus service. They became convinced that the property was at risk of collapse and evicted Lyttle from his home in 2006. He died four years later, leaving no apparent heirs, while the council attempted to shore up the building by pouring in tonnes of aerated concrete.

'The Mole House intrigued me because it had the same type of epochal quality to it as the Dirty House and had really become engrained as a piece of London's archaeology,' explains Adjaye. 'We had to negotiate what it was that we should hold onto, what we had to let go of, and what we had to establish new relations with.'

After Lyttle's death in 2010, the house was put up for auction. Webster placed a successful bid and began planning her new home and studio.

'I am a bit of a hoarder, being an artist, but the Mole Man was on a different scale,' says Webster. 'When the council turned up with a cement mixer...they just filled up the house, the garden and everything. But they hadn't bothered to clear the house first so when we had to dig everything out, we would find a shopping trolley embedded in there or a door on its own standing up. It was like Pompeii.'

The boundary wall was rebuilt in reclaimed brick and the house carefully stabilized, while preserving remnants and markers of Lyttle's

Left The sitting room, dining area and kitchen are found within the elevated piano nobile at mid-level; the 'Puppy' vase on the circular table is by Jeff Koons (b. 1955).

Below The bespoke kitchen is located alongside the main seating area. Its shelves hold a collection of sculptures by Sue Webster and Tim Noble.

Opposite While the study area and master bathroom are on the uppermost storey of the house, Webster's double-height studio is situated in the new basement level. The high white wall features Webster's 'crime scene' documenting her teenage preoccupation with Siouxsie and the Banshees, along with their contemporaries, also recorded in Webster's book, *I Was a Teenage Banshee*.

Below The studio has direct connections with the surrounding outdoor spaces, as seen in this route to the front garden via an undercroft that holds remnants and relics from the Mole Man's famous excavations.

excavations. A spacious double-height studio was created at basement and lower-ground-floor level, supported by a great concrete cruciform that Adjaye inserted in the heart of the building, along with fresh foundation, piers and floor plates. The raw concrete contrasts with the textural patina of the restored façade, while Webster decided to coat two of the windows to the street with layers of mirrored vinyl. This allows the occupants to see out, but adds to the enigmatic quality of the exterior.

Inside, the house is arranged over the upper two levels, where the raw concrete contrasts with plastered walls and wooden floors. Most elements here are bespoke, including the kitchen and library wall in the open-plan living space. A wooden staircase leads up to the bedrooms and bathrooms on the top storey, as well as a study area on the landing topped by a vast, operable skylight that gives the space the feel of a sunken courtyard when opened.

'If you just tear these monuments down then there is no legacy for future generations,' says Webster. 'It was such a fascinating story to begin with, and we wanted to add another layer to it. I like working with people like David; we dare one another to go one step further and there are no boundaries.'

NOTES

All quotes that are not attributed below are from interviews by the author with the client or architect.

1. Stamp 2012, p. 76.
2. Muthesius 1979, pp. 49–51.
3. Macaulay 1994, p. 13.
4. Davey 1995, p. 99.
5. Reading and Coe 1992, p. 45.
6. Allan 1992, p. 182.
7. Sharp and Rendel 2008, p. 25.
8. Ibid., p. 119.
9. 'Geoffrey Walford, A Client on His House: 66 Frognal', *RIBA Journal*, 19 December 1938, p. 185.
10. Klein 2020, pp. 22–23.
11. Rowan Moore, 'Peter Womersley: From Bauhaus to Boiler House', *The Observer*, 22 January 2017.
12. Mark Girouard, 'Old and New in Harmony', *Country Life*, 26 October 1961, p. 1018.
13. John Pardey, 'Notes on the Spence House', Project Descriptions, 2000, p. 1.
14. Edwards 1995, p. 82.
15. Hugh Pearman, 'Probably the Best Modern House in the World', *The Sunday Times*, 3 February 2008.
16. 'Creek Vean House', Foster + Partners website. Accessed by the author 7 April 2023, www.fosterandpartners.com/projects/creek-vean-house.
17. All quotes from an interview with the author.
18. John Partridge, '8 Houses Through One Pair of Eyes', *Architectural Review*, September 1971.
19. Ibid.
20. Historic England Listing 1413746, 18.9.13.
21. Charles Jencks, 'Star-Struck House', *House & Garden* (US), April 1985, p. 207.
22. Ibid., p. 114.
23. Anthony Hudson, 'Baggy House: Underlying Concepts', Project Descriptions, 1994, p. 2.
24. Ros Drinkwater, 'Biorhythm', *House & Garden*, November 1999, p. 126.
25. Jonathan Glancey, 'In Britain, Money and Marketing Are What Matter Most', *The Guardian*, 21 November 2005.
26. William Mann, *Inhabiting the Ruin: Work at Astley Castle* (London: Witherford Watson Mann Architects, 2016), pp. 8–9.
27. Ibid., pp. 28–29.
28. Ibid., p. 29.
29. Ellie Stakhaki, 'Step Inside David Adjaye and Sue Webster's Mole House', *Wallpaper** online. Accessed by the author 7 April 2023. www.wallpaper.com/architecture/mole-house-sue-webster-david-adjaye-london.

SELECT BIBLIOGRAPHY

Allan, John, *Lubetkin: Architecture and the Tradition of Progress* (London: RIBA Publishing, 1992)
———, *Berthold Lubetkin* (London: Merrell, 2002)
Allison, Peter (ed.), *David Adjaye: Houses* (London: Thames & Hudson, 2005)
———, *Adjaye: Works 1995–2007* (London: Thames & Hudson, 2020)
Andrews, Peter, et al., *The House Book* (London: Phaidon, 2001)
Aslet, Clive, *The Arts & Crafts Country House* (London: Aurum Press, 2011)
Betsky, Aaron, *Landscrapers: Building with the Land* (London: Thames & Hudson, 2002)
Bradbury, Dominic, *The Timeless Home: James Gorst Architects* (London: Lund Humphries, 2019)
———, *Nick Eldridge: Unique Houses* (London: Lund Humphries, 2022)
Breward, Christopher, & Ghislaine Wood (eds), *British Design from 1948: Innovation in the Modern Age* (London: V&A Publishing, 2012)
Brown, Jane, *A Garden & Three Houses* (Haddenham: Turn End Charitable Trust, 2010)
Byars, Mel, *The Design Encyclopedia* (London: Laurence King, 2004)
Charlton, Susannah, & Elain Harwood (eds), *100 Houses 100 Years* (London: Batsford, 2017)
Chipperfield, David, et al., *David Chipperfield Architects* (London: Thames & Hudson, 2013)
Cobbers, Arnt, *Marcel Breuer* (Cologne: Taschen, 2007)
Crinson, Mark, *Alison and Peter Smithson* (Swindon: Historic England, 2018)
Davey, Peter, *Arts and Crafts Architecture* (London: Phaidon, 1995)
Davies, Colin, *Key Houses of the Twentieth Century* (London: Laurence King, 2006)
Davies, Colin, Patrick Hodgkinson & Kenneth Frampton, *Hopkins: The Work of Michael Hopkins and Partners* (London: Phaidon, 1995)
Donati, Cristina, *Michael Hopkins* (Milan: Skira, 2006)
Doordan, Dennis P., *Twentieth-Century Architecture* (London: Laurence King, 2001)
Driller, Joachim, *Breuer Houses* (London: Phaidon, 2000)
Droste, Magdalena, *Bauhaus* (Cologne: Taschen, 2006)
Edwards, Brian, *Basil Spence: 1907–1976* (Maidenhead: Rutland Press, 1995)
———, *Goddards: Sir Edwin Lutyens* (London: Phaidon, 1996)
Field, Marcus, *Future Systems* (London: Phaidon, 1999)

Fiell, Charlotte & Peter, *Design of the Twentieth Century* (Cologne: Taschen, 1999)
Frampton, Kenneth, *Modern Architecture: A Critical History*, 4th ed. (London: Thames & Hudson, 2007)
Franklin, Geraint, & Elain Harwood, *Post-Modern Buildings in Britain* (London: Batsford, 2017)
Futagawa, Yukio (ed.), *GA Houses Special: Masterpieces, 1945–1970* (Tokyo: ADA Edita, 2001)
———, *GA Houses Special: Masterpieces, 1971–2000* (Tokyo: ADA Edita, 2001)
Glancey, Jonathan, *Twentieth-Century Architecture* (London: Carlton, 1998)
Gössel, Peter, & Gabriele Leuthäuser, *Architecture in the 20th Century* (Cologne: Taschen, 2005)
Gura, Judith, *Postmodern Design Complete* (London: Thames & Hudson, 2017)
Harwood, Elain, & James O. Davies, *England's Post-War Listed Buildings* (London: Batsford, 2015)
Heathcote, Edwin, with Charles Jencks, *The Cosmic House* (London: Jencks Foundation, 2021)
Hitchmough, Wendy, *C. F. A. Voysey* (London: Phaidon, 1995)
———, *C. F. A. Voysey: The Homestead* (London: Phaidon, 1994)
Jencks, Charles, *The Post-Modern Reader* (London: Academy Editions, 1992)
Jodidio, Philip, *Sir Norman Foster* (Cologne: Taschen, 1997)
Klein, Shelley, *The See-Through House: My Father in Full Colour* (London: Chatto & Windus, 2020)
Long, Philip, & Jane Thomas (eds), *Basil Spence: Architect* (Edinburgh: National Galleries of Scotland, 2007)
Macaulay, James, *Hill House: Charles Rennie Mackintosh* (London: Phaidon, 1994)
Morris, Alison, *Plain Space: John Pawson* (London: Phaidon, 2010)
Muthesius, Hermann, *The English House* (Oxford: BSP Professional Books, 1979)
Pevsner, Nikolaus, *Pioneers of Modern Design*, 4th ed. (New Haven: Yale University Press, 2005)
Postiglione, Gennaro (ed.), *One Hundred Houses for One Hundred Architects* (Cologne: Taschen, 2004)
Powell, Kenneth, *Richard Rogers: Complete Works*, vols 1–3 (London: Phaidon, 1999–2006)
Powers, Alan, *Modern: The Modern Movement in Britain* (London: Merrell, 2005)
Reading, Malcolm, & Peter Coe, *Lubetkin & Tecton* (London: Triangle Architectural Publishing, 1992)
Richardson, Phyllis, *Skywood House & The Architecture of Graham Phillips* (London: Thames & Hudson, 2014)
Rybczynski, Witold, *Home: A Short History of an Idea* (London: Penguin, 1987)

Sharp, Dennis, & Sally Rendel, *Connell Ward & Lucas: Modern Movement Architects in England, 1929–1939* (London: Frances Lincoln, 2008)
Stamp, Gavin, *Edwin Lutyens: Country Houses* (London: Aurum Press, 2012)
Sudjic, Deyan, *Home: The Twentieth-Century House* (London: Laurence King, 1999)
———, *John Pawson: Works* (London: Phaidon, 2005)
———, *Future Systems* (London: Phaidon, 2006)
Tinniswood, Adrian, *The Art Deco House* (London: Mitchell Beazley, 2002)
Van Den Heuvel, Dirk, & Max Risselada, *Alison & Peter Smithson: From the House of the Future to a House of Today* (Rotterdam: 010 Publishers, 2004)
Watkin, David, *A History of Western Architecture* (London: Laurence King, 1986)
Weaver, Lawrence (ed.), *Small Country Houses of To-Day* (London: Country Life, 1922)
Welsh, John, *Modern House* (London: Phaidon, 1995)
Weston, Richard, *Modernism* (London: Phaidon, 2001)
———, *The House in the Twentieth Century* (London: Laurence King, 2002)
———, *Key Buildings of the Twentieth Century* (London: Laurence King, 2004)
Wilk, Christopher (ed.), *Modernism: Designing a New World* (London: V&A Publishing, 2006)

BIOGRAPHIES

DAVID ADJAYE (b. 1966)
Adjaye was born in Tanzania, the son of a Ghanaian diplomat. The family moved to London and Adjaye studied at South Bank University and the Royal College of Art. He co-founded his first practice with William Russell in 1994 and then opened his own London studio in 2000. Many of Adjaye's projects involve collaborations with artists such as Chris Ofili and Olafur Eliasson. Since the completion of the Museum of Contemporary Art in Denver (2007), Adjaye's work has become increasingly international in scope. The Smithsonian National Museum of African American History and Culture in Washington, DC (2016) is one of his largest projects to date. **www.adjaye.com**

POVL AHM (1926–2005)
Danish structural engineer Ahm was born in Aarhus and studied in Copenhagen. In 1952 he joined the London office of Ove Arup & Partners, working with architects such as Basil Spence, Arne Jacobsen and Jørn Utzon, who designed the Ahm family home in Hertfordshire (see p. 115).

PETER ALDINGTON (b. 1933)
Born in Preston, Aldington studied at Manchester University's School of Architecture, qualifying in 1956. He worked with London County Council's architecture department and then the Timber Research Development Association before founding his own practice in 1963. With his wife Margaret, he completed Turn End and its two neighbouring residences in 1968 (see p. 121). John Craig joined the practice as a partner in 1970 and then Paul Collinge. Aldington is best known for his residential work, which fuses Modernist principles, vernacular references and local materials.
www.turnend.org.uk

MACKAY HUGH BAILLIE SCOTT (1865–1945)
Born in Kent to a farming family of Scottish descent, Baillie Scott initially studied agriculture before moving into architecture. He was apprenticed to Charles Davis, Bath's city architect, and then moved to the Isle of Man to set up his own practice in 1889, followed by relocation to Bedfordshire. By the 1890s, Baillie Scott's architectural work was in great demand. Large-scale commissions were mixed with more modest designs, all within a refined Arts and Crafts style. As well as Blackwell (see p. 21) key residences included the White House in Helensburgh, Scotland (1900) and Waldbühl in Uzwil, Switzerland (1914).

MEREDITH BOWLES (b. 1963)
Bowles studied at the University of Sheffield, the Royal College of Art and the Architectural Association. He established Mole Architects in Cambridgeshire in 1997 and was later joined by director Ian Bramwell. Sustainable design has always been a cornerstone of the practice, which has devoted much of its attention to houses and housing, as well as serving as a consultant to Alain de Botton's Living Architecture collective. Recent Mole projects include the Design District D2 in Greenwich (2021) and the Marmalade Lane co-housing scheme in Cambridge (2019).
www.molearchitects.co.uk

PATRICK BRADLEY (b. 1980)
Having grown up on the family farm in rural County Londonderry, Bradley studied architecture at Queen's University in Belfast. He worked with a conservation-led practice in Belfast before joining McGurk Architects. Bradley established his own company in 2010, winning acclaim with the design of Grillagh Water House in Maghera (see p. 243), situated on the family farm, and has largely specialized in residential work since then. Bradley balances practising architecture with a role as a judge and presenter on television shows.
pb-architects.com

MARCEL BREUER (1902–1981)
Born in Hungary, Breuer studied in Vienna and then at the Bauhaus under Walter Gropius. He went on to become a master at the Bauhaus in Dessau, where he began developing furniture designs and working on the interiors of the masters' houses. In 1928 he launched his own architectural practice in Berlin. In 1935 he emigrated to London and worked in partnership with F. R. S. Yorke while also developing furniture designs at Isokon. Gropius then offered him a teaching post at Harvard, where the two friends also collaborated on a number of residential projects. In 1941 Breuer founded his own practice, which was based in New York from 1946, with his post-war work including major projects such as the UNESCO Headquarters in Paris (1958, with Pier Luigi Nervi and Bernard Zehrfuss) and the Whitney Museum of American Art in New York (1966).

BRINKWORTH
Based in London, Brinkworth design consultancy was established in 1990 by founding partner and CEO Adam Brinkworth with director/partner Kevin Brennan joining a few years later. Their early work focused on the retail and fashion sectors, before expanding into residential work and housing, including (in association with Ben Kelly) the regeneration of Park Hill housing complex in Sheffield. The practice, which is involved in interiors, architecture and brand design, opened a New York office in 2017.
brinkworth.com

JANE BURNSIDE (b. 1965)
Burnside grew up in County Londonderry and studied architecture at the universities of Manchester and Bath, where she was taught by Peter Aldington (see p. 121). She went on to study with the British School in Rome and to work in the USA with Michael Graves. Returning to Northern Ireland, Burnside worked with Robinson McIlwaine Architects in Belfast before establishing her own practice in 1990, as well as teaching at Queen's University in Belfast. Much of her work has focused on private residential projects, particularly original country houses, including her own home.
www.janedburnsidearchitects.co.uk

DAVID CHIPPERFIELD (b. 1953)
Born in London, Chipperfield studied at Kingston School of Art and the Architectural Association. He worked with both Richard Rogers (see p. 133) and Norman Foster before founding his own practice in 1985. Key projects in the UK include the River and Rowing Museum in Henley-on-Thames (1997), the Hepworth in Wakefield (2011) and Turner Contemporary in Margate (2011). His practice has also built

a considerable portfolio internationally, such as Des Moines Public Library in Iowa (2006), Neues Museum in Berlin (2009) and Museo Jumex in Mexico City (2013).
davidchipperfield.com

TREVOR DANNATT (1920–2021)
Dannatt was born in London and studied at Regent Street Polytechnic. In 1943 he joined Jane Drew and Maxwell Fry's office, and five years later joined the architecture department of the London County Council, where he was part of the team working on the Royal Festival Hall (1951). Soon afterwards Dannatt founded his own practice and balanced residential work (see p. 85), with university campus projects and other commissions, such as the Quaker Meeting House in Blackheath (1972). Dannatt was also an exhibition curator and writer, whose publications included *Modern Architecture in Britain* (Batsford, 1959).

JAMES DUNBAR-NASMITH (1927–2023)
Dunbar-Smith was born in England but always maintained a close relationship with Scotland through his mother and her family, who were from Morayshire. He studied architecture at the University of Cambridge followed by Edinburgh University and later joined Robert Hogg Matthew's practice in the city. In 1957 he and a work colleague, Graham Couper Law, decided to form their own practice, becoming well known for both residential work and theatre design, including the Eden Court Theatre in Inverness (1976).

NICK ELDRIDGE (b. 1957)
Eldridge attended the University of Liverpool and then London's Architectural Association. He joined Foster + Partners while still a student and continued with the practice after completing his studies, before moving on to Troughton McAslan. In 1998 Eldridge and a colleague formed Eldridge Smerin, and their first residential project, The Lawns in Highgate, was shortlisted for the Stirling Prize in 2001. In 2015, Eldridge rebranded his practice Eldridge London and, later, created a studio in Cornwall known as Eldridge Newlyn. Key projects include Greenways (see p. 273) and Garden House in Highgate (2021).
eldridgelondon.com

TERRY FARRELL (b. 1938)
Born in Cheshire, Farrell read architecture at Newcastle University's School of Architecture and urban planning at the University of Pennsylvania, Philadelphia. He formed a partnership with Nicholas Grimshaw in London in 1965 and then, in 1980, established Terry Farrell & Partners. Some of Farrell's projects sit within the High Tech tradition of British architecture; others are categorized as Postmodern,

such as his landmark MI6 Headquarters in London (1994). Other projects include the Deep aquarium in Hull (2002), Beijing South Railway Station (2008) and the KK100 skyscraper in Shenzhen, China (2011).
farrells.com

FAT ARCHITECTURE
Fashion Architecture Taste, or FAT, was established in 1995 by architects and designers Charles Holland, Sean Griffiths and Sam Jacob, with a multidisciplinary approach spanning architecture, urban design and interiors. In the architectural realm, projects include housing for Urban Splash in Islington Square (2006) and the extension of Thornton Heath Library (2010). A House for Essex (see p. 249), designed in conjunction with Grayson Perry, was the practice's last project before the three partners went their separate ways.
www.fashionarchitecturetaste.com

PETER FOGGO (1930–1993)
Foggo studied at the University of Liverpool, where he met his future practice partner David Thomas. They formed Foggo & Thomas in 1959, and were best known for a series of pioneering standalone houses built during the early 1960s using innovative structural frameworks. The two friends then joined Arup Associates, where Foggo became a partner and director. In 1989, he left Arup to set up Peter Foggo Associates, which continued after his death under the name Foggo Associates.
www.foggo.com

FOSTER LOMAS
London-based practice Foster Lomas was co-founded in 2005 by Greg Lomas and Will Foster. Lomas studied architecture at Brighton University and London Metropolitan University; he was a team member of three practices before establishing Foster Lomas. Foster studied interior architecture at the University of Wales in Cardiff and at London Metropolitan University before working on the Wembley Stadium project; he was also part of the team at Patel Taylor. Much of the practice's recent work, including Sartfell Restorative Rural Retreat (see p. 297), has focused on innovative residential projects.
fosterlomas.com

RICHARD FOUND (b. 1966)
Found studied at the University of North London, followed by time with David Davies Associates and Johnson Naylor. He established Found Associates in 1997 with an early focus on architecture and interiors for retail and fashion clients in London, New York and elsewhere, as well as offices and restaurants. Residential work has become an important sector for the practice, with several country-house new

builds in England and the Channel Islands, as well as multiple projects in London. **foundassociates.com**

FUTURE SYSTEMS
Future Systems was an innovative architectural partnership led by Jan Kaplický (1937–2009) and Amanda Levete (b. 1955). Kaplický was born in Prague and worked in private practice there before moving to the UK in 1968, working in the offices of Denys Lasdun, Richard Rogers and Norman Foster before co-founding Future Systems in 1979. Born in Bridgend, Levete studied at the Architectural Association in London and worked with Will Alsop and Richard Rogers before becoming a partner at Future Systems in 1989. Projects include the Media Centre at Lord's Cricket Ground in London (1999) and Selfridges, Birmingham (2003).

JAMES GORST (b. 1950)
Gorst grew up in rural Suffolk, where his father was a chief planning officer. He studied history at the University of Cambridge followed by architecture. Gorst worked with Denys Lasdun and John Outram before establishing his own practice in 1981. Much of his early work involved the restoration of period Georgian houses before beginning work on an influential sequence of new-build country houses, including Whithurst Lodge in Sussex (2001), and Hannington Farm (see p. 291). James Gorst Architects is led by its principal and director David Roy. **jamesgorstarchitects.com**

OLIVER HILL (1887–1968)
During the early years of his career, Hill was much influenced by mentor Edwin Lutyens and the Arts and Crafts movement. But during the 1930s he embraced Modernism and began designing a series of forward-thinking houses and hotels infused with touches of Art Deco streamlining and styling. Projects include the Midland Hotel in Morecombe (1933), Cherry Hill (see p. 55) and a series of new houses in Frinton-on-Sea, Essex. Hill also designed the British Pavilion for the Paris Expo of 1937.

MICHAEL (b. 1935) and PATTY (b. 1942) HOPKINS
The son of a builder, Michael Hopkins studied at the Architectural Association and worked in the office of Basil Spence before going into partnership with Norman Foster. He went on to co-found Hopkins Architects alongside his wife Patty Hopkins in 1976, with the practice soon establishing itself as a leading light in the High Tech movement. An initial emphasis on structural and technological innovation was augmented by an interest in contextuality and the reinterpretation of

more traditional materials. Projects include Glyndebourne Opera House in East Sussex (1994) and Portcullis House, London (1999). **www.hopkins.co.uk**

HUDSON ARCHITECTS
Born in Norfolk, Anthony Hudson (b. 1955) studied architecture at the universities of Cambridge and Westminster. He worked for a number of practices in India and London before founding his own practice in 1985. He later joined forces with architect Sarah Featherstone before re-forming his own practice in 2002 with the creation of Hudson Architects. Hudson Architects has made its greatest impact to date through a series of crafted and considered private houses and conversions, as well as larger cultural and educational projects, including multiple buildings for Norwich University of the Arts. **hudsonarchitects.co.uk**

CHARLES JENCKS (1939–2019)
Jencks, an architect, designer, landscape designer, lecturer, writer and theorist, was born in the USA. He studied at Harvard University and completed his PhD, under the supervision of Reyner Banham, at University College London. Jencks became one of the leading proponents of Postmodernism, not only through his work as a designer but also in his scholarly work, which included the landmark book *The Language of Post-Modern Architecture* (1977). Later in his career, Jencks concentrated on landscape design, including his own Garden of Cosmic Speculation in Dumfriesshire. He was also co-founder of the Maggie's Cancer Centres, named after his second wife, garden designer Maggie Keswick Jencks. **www.charlesjencks.com**

LILY JENCKS (b. 1980)
Jencks, daughter of Charles Jencks and Maggie Keswick Jencks (see above), grew up in London and Scotland. She studied at Columbia University and the University of Pennsylvania, and then worked with Gehry Partners and OMA. She founded Lily Jencks Studio in 2010 and also began collaborating with her father on a number of projects in 2011 (as JencksSquared). Her work includes the courtyard garden at Maggie's Gartnavel in Glasgow (2011, with architecture by Rem Koolhaas and OMA) and Ruins Studio, designed in conjunction with Nathanael Dorent (see p. 267). In 2021 Jencks became the director of the Jencks Foundation at The Cosmic House in London (see p. 157). **www.lilyjencksstudio.com**

KEMP & TASKER
Leslie Kemp (1899–1997) and Frederick E. Tasker were best known for a series of Art Deco cinemas, mostly built in and around

London during the 1930s. These included Odeon cinemas in Chadwell Heath, Greenwich and Romford as well as the Ritz Cinema in Luton. Other projects comprised residential commissions and motor-car showrooms. They also exhibited a house at the Ideal Home Show in 1934 at the 'Village of Tomorrow', which was reproduced in a number of locations in the UK and Ireland. Kemp later relocated to Canada, where he specialized in cinema design.

BERTHOLD LUBETKIN (1901–1990)
Born in Georgia, Lubetkin studied initially in Moscow just after the Russian Revolution, followed by Berlin and Paris, where he worked in the studio of Auguste Perret. He moved to London in 1931 and one year later co-founded Tecton. Lubetkin designed a series of sculptural zoo buildings in reinforced concrete, including the Penguin Pool (1934) at London Zoo, as well as two London apartment buildings, Highpoint I and II (1935 and 1938). One of the architect's last pre-war projects was Finsbury Health Centre of 1938. Post-war projects focused on social housing, yet Lubetkin soon became disillusioned by British conservatism and eventually retreated from architecture.

COLIN LUCAS (1906–1984)
Lucas came from an avant-garde family, with his mother a composer and his father an inventor and entrepreneur. He studied at the University of Cambridge and then worked as an architect-builder experimenting with concrete construction; Noah's House (1934) in Buckinghamshire was among his early projects. He joined forces with New Zealanders Basil Ward and Amyas Connell in 1934 to form Connell, Ward & Lucas. The practice was short lived, lasting until just 1939, but it was highly influential, and with a series of innovative houses the trio established a powerful British variant on the International Style. After World War II Lucas joined London County Council architect's department.

EDWIN LUTYENS (1869–1944)
Lutyens set up his own practice in 1889, after an apprenticeship with country house architects George & Peto. His work varied between Neoclassical grandeur and Arts and Crafts buildings, initially influenced by Norman Shaw, William Morris and Philip Webb. Within the UK he was best known for a series of highly influential country houses – Deanery Gardens in Berkshire (1902) and Castle Drogo in Devon (1930) – and the Cenotaph memorial (1920). He famously took his career to a new level with his work in planning imperial New Delhi and some of its most striking buildings, including the Viceroy's House (1931). **www.lutyenstrust.org.uk**

CHARLES RENNIE MACKINTOSH (1868–1928)
Born in Glasgow, Mackintosh spent his most productive years in the city, famously designing the Glasgow School of Art in two phases (1899 and 1909). He forged a unique style that combined Arts and Crafts influences with Art Nouveau, Scottish vernacular references and a progressive modernity. Much of his best-known work, including Willow Tea Rooms in Glasgow (1904) and Hill House (see p. 27), involved collaborations with his wife, artist Margaret Macdonald Mackintosh (1864–1933). The couple left Glasgow in 1914, with Mackintosh largely abandoning architecture and developing his furniture designs as well as painting watercolours. **www.crmsociety.com**

MICHAEL MANSER (1929–2016)
Manser studied at Regent Street Polytechnic, now part of the University of Westminster. He worked initially with Norman & Dawbarn before founding his own firm in 1960. Among Manser's key early projects were the Waterlooville Baptist Church in Hampshire (1967) and Capel Manor (see p. 145). Manser served as president of the Royal Institute of British Architects (RIBA) from 1983 to 1985, and the Manser Medal for the best newly completed house in the UK was launched in his honour in 2001. The Manser Practice is now run by his son, Jonathan Manser. **www.manser.co.uk**

ALEX MICHAELIS (b. 1965)
The son of an architect, Michaelis studied architecture at Oxford Brookes University and, in 1991, began working at Julyan Wickham's practice. With Tim Boyd, he co-founded Michaelis Boyd in 1996. Residential work is an important part of the practice's portfolio, including Michaelis's own homes. Work in the hospitality sector comprises Soho Farmhouse in Oxfordshire (2015) and the Williamsburg Hotel in New York (2017), while other large-scale projects include a collection of apartments at Battersea Power Station (2021). **www.michaelisboyd.com**

RICHARD MURPHY (b. 1955)
Murphy studied at the universities of Newcastle and Edinburgh before establishing his own practice in Edinburgh in 1991. In 1996, Murphy designed the first Maggie's Centre; the project was nominated for the Stirling Prize in 1997. Other projects include Dundee Contemporary Arts (1999) and the British High Commission in Sri Lanka (2008). In 2016, Murphy's own home in Edinburgh was awarded RIBA's House of the Year prize. **www.richardmurphyarchitects.com**

ROBIN PARTINGTON (b. 1960)

Partington studied at the University of Liverpool and joined Foster + Partners in 1984. He was with the firm, where he became a director, for seventeen years with projects including the American Air Museum at Duxford (1997) and Hong Kong International Airport (1998). In 2001, he joined Hamiltons Architects before founding his own practice, Apt, in 2009. Apt works across a wide range of sectors, such as housing, placemaking and recreation. Projects include Park House (2012) and Chapter House (2019), both in London, as well as Holmewood (see p. 201).
apt.london

JOHN PAWSON (b. 1949)

Born in Yorkshire, Pawson travelled and taught in Japan for a number of years after working in his family's textile business. He then studied at the Architectural Association in London and founded his own practice in 1981, with early projects including an apartment for writer Bruce Chatwin (1982). Pawson formed a brief partnership with Claudio Silvestrin from 1987 to 1989, collaborating on the Neuendorf House in Mallorca (1989). Other projects are Tilty Barn in Essex (1995) and Nový Dvůr Monastery in the Czech Republic (2004). Pawson's many books on architecture, design and food have been highly influential.
www.johnpawson.com

GRAYSON PERRY (b. 1960)

Artist, ceramicist, author and presenter, Perry studied fine art at Portsmouth College of Art & Design. He has exhibited his work across the UK and internationally and began presenting documentaries for Channel 4 in 2005. Working with FAT Architecture, Perry designed A House for Essex for Living Architecture (see p. 249), with the project also leading to an associated touring exhibition entitled 'Julie Cope's Grand Tour'.

GRAHAM PHILLIPS (b. 1947)

Phillips studied at the University of Liverpool, joining Foster + Partners in 1975. Early projects included the IBM Technical Park and HSBC Headquarters (1986), followed by Hong Kong International Airport (1998). In 1993 he became managing director and then chief executive officer. Phillips retired from the practice in 2008 to concentrate on his own projects, among which are Skywood (see p. 183) and residential projects in London and Mallorca.
www.skywoodhouse.com/graham-phillips

E. S. PRIOR (1852–1932)

Educated at the University of Cambridge, where he was a prize-winning athlete,

Prior went to work for his mentor, Norman Shaw, in 1874. Six years later he founded his own London practice. Prior was also a scholar and theorist, writing key accounts of Gothic art and architecture, and was the co-founder of the Art Workers' Guild. In later years he became the Slade Professor of Fine Art at Cambridge and founded the Cambridge School of Architecture. His architectural portfolio primarily combined residential work with ecclesiastical and educational projects, including Cambridge Medical Schools (1904) and St Andrew's Church in Roker, Sunderland (1907).

ADAM RICHARDS (b. 1967)

Richards studied architecture at the University of Cambridge and worked with architects Niall McLaughlin and O'Donnell + Tuomey. He founded his own practice in the year 2000 with key projects including Ditchling Museum of Art + Craft in Sussex (2013), Walmer Castle Learning Centre and Café in Kent (2019) and his own family home, Nithurst Farm (see p. 285).
www.adamrichards.co.uk

RICHARD ROGERS (1933–2021)

Born in Florence, Rogers moved to London as a child. He studied at the Architectural Association and then at Yale School of Architecture, under Serge Chermayeff, where he met Norman Foster. The two co-founded the short-lived Team 4 practice in 1963. In 1971, along with Renzo Piano, Rogers won the competition to build the Pompidou Centre and he founded Richard Rogers Partnership in 1977, now known as Rogers Stirk Harbour + Partners. Key projects include Lloyd's of London (1986), the Millennium Dome in Greenwich (1999), the National Assembly for Wales in Cardiff (2005) and Barajas Airport in Madrid (2005).
rshp.com

SEELY & PAGET

John Seely (1900–1963) and Paul Paget (1901–1985) met at Trinity College, Cambridge, and formed a joint practice in 1926, based in London. Seely became Baron Mottistone and their society connections helped in sourcing a number of their early residential commissions. Later, they specialized in ecclesiastical architecture, working on the reconstruction of various London churches damaged in World War II, with Paget ultimately becoming chief surveyor at St Paul's Cathedral. Seely & Paget's many churches include the Chapel of the Venerable Bede in Durham (1939) and St Mary's Church in Islington (1955).

DAVID SHELLEY (1934–2012)

Shelley was based in West Bridgford, Nottingham, and was responsible for the design of a number of notable mid-century houses in Nottinghamshire and

neighbouring counties. These included Adila (see p. 139), Morley House in Derbyshire (1974) and Monchen House in Nottinghamshire (1978).

KEN SHUTTLEWORTH (b. 1952)

Born in Birmingham, Shuttleworth studied architecture at the University of Leicester and then joined Norman Foster's practice. He became a partner in 1991 and collaborated on the design of 30 St Mary Axe, or 'the Gherkin' (2004). He founded his own practice, Make, in 2004 and quickly developed a diverse portfolio of projects in the UK and internationally, characterized by a dynamic and innovative approach to form and structure. Key projects include the new neighbourhood of Chobham Manor in East London (2019) and Brookfield Place in Sydney (2021).
www.makearchitects.com

SKENE CATLING DE LA PEÑA

Skene Catling de la Peña was established by Charlotte Skene Catling and Jaime de la Peña in 2003. They met as students at the University of Westminster and began collaborating on projects using a highly contextual 'geoarchaeological' approach, as seen in Dairy House in Somerset (2008) and Flint House (see p. 255). The practice has offices in London and Madrid while also creating opportunities for the principals to pursue other interests, including teaching, writing and solo projects.
scdlp.net

ALISON (1928–1993) and PETER (1923–2003) SMITHSON

Born in Sheffield and Stockton-on-Tees respectively, the two architects met at the School of Architecture in Newcastle. They founded a practice together in 1950, having won their first and one of their most important commissions, Hunstanton School in Norfolk (1954). Flamboyant and outspoken, the Smithsons won great praise for their Economist Building in London (1964) and significant criticism for their Brutalist Robin Hood Gardens housing scheme in East London (1972). As curators and cultural commentators, they were closely allied with the development of Pop Art in the UK in the 1960s.

BASIL SPENCE (1907–1976)

Born in India, Spence studied in Edinburgh and London, working initially for Edwin Lutyens. He co-founded his first practice in Scotland, with his work influenced by the Arts and Crafts movement, before serving in the British Army during World War II. He founded Spence & Partners in the 1940s, working in a distinctly Modernist and sometimes Brutalist style. His crowning achievement was Coventry Cathedral (1962). Later work placed Spence on the

international stage, as seen in the executive wing of the New Zealand Parliament Buildings in Wellington (1964) and the British Embassy in Rome (1971).

SETH STEIN ARCHITECTS

Born in New York, Seth Stein (b. 1959) grew up in London, studying architecture at the University of Manchester and the Architectural Association in London. He worked with both Richard Rogers and Norman Foster before establishing Seth Stein Architects in London in 1990. Much of the practice's work has focused on new-build private houses, particularly in rural and coastal settings in Finland, South Africa and Australia.
www.sethstein.com

TEAM 4

The architectural practice Team 4 was founded in 1963 by Richard Rogers, Norman Foster and Su Rogers (née Brumwell), who had studied together at Yale University, along with Wendy Foster (née Cheesman). The practice existed for four years, with key projects including the Reliance Controls Centre in Swindon (1967) and Creek Vean in Cornwall (see p. 127).

JØRN UTZON (1918–2008)

Danish architect Utzon was born in Copenhagen, establishing his own practice there in 1945. In 1957 Utzon won the Sydney Opera House competition, although the project proved controversial and he resigned from the job in 1966, with completion following in 1973. The building was declared a World Heritage site in 2007, and Utzon was awarded the Pritzker Prize in 2003. Other influential projects include Utzon's family house in Helsingør, Denmark (1952) and his two family houses on the island of Mallorca, Can Lis (1972) and Can Feliz (1994).

CHARLES VOYSEY (1857–1941)

Voysey was educated by his father and private tutors before being articled to architect J. P. Seddon in 1873. He then worked with George Devey's office before founding his own practice in 1882, later becoming a friend and neighbour of fellow Arts and Crafts practitioner E. S. Prior. The prolific architect made a significant impact with a series of country houses and cottages, while also designing textiles and furniture. Among Voysey's most influential houses are his own home, The Orchard, in Hertfordshire (1899), and two houses in the Lake District: Broadleys (1898) and Moorcrag (1898).
www.voyseysociety.org

SUE WEBSTER (b. 1967)

Webster took a fine art foundation

course at Leicester Polytechnic before
going on to study fine art at Nottingham
Trent University. She established herself
as an artist with abstract sculptures,
assemblages and other artworks conceived
in partnership with Tim Noble, before
developing her solo career with a series
of exhibitions and publications. Webster's
first residential project with Adjaye was
Dirty House in Shoreditch (2002) before
undertaking Mole House (see p. 309).

WITHERFORD WATSON MANN

Witherford Watson Mann was co-founded
in 2002 by Stephen Witherford, Christopher
Watson and William Mann. All three
architects studied at the University of
Cambridge, and all three graduated in 1991.
Key projects include Astley Castle (see
p. 237), which won the Stirling Prize in 2013,
Nevill Holt Opera in Leicestershire (2018)
and Courtauld Connects at the Courtauld
Gallery, London (2021).
www.wwmarchitects.co.uk

PETER WOMERSLEY (1923–1993)

Womersley trained at the Architectural
Association after wartime military service,
graduating in 1952. Soon afterwards he
established his own practice, based in
Scotland, and became known for a series of
highly accomplished mid-century houses,
including Farnley Hey in West Yorkshire
(1954), High Sunderland (see p. 79) and
the Gala Fairydean Stadium in Galashiels
(1964). In addition to his projects in the
UK, Womersley worked in Hong Kong and
was based there from 1978 onwards.
preserving-womersley.net

PETER ZUMTHOR (b. 1943)

Born in Basel, Switzerland, Zumthor
trained as a designer and architect at the
Kunstgewerbeschule Basel and at the Pratt
Institute in New York. He established his
own practice in Haldenstein, Switzerland,
in 1979. Major Swiss projects include the
St Benedict Chapel in Sumvitg (1988),
the Thermal Baths in Vals (1996) and the
Kunsthaus Bregenz (1997), while he has
also worked in Germany and the UK.
zumthor.org

GAZETTEER

This listing contains contact details
for houses that are accessible to the
public, either for visits, special events
or holiday rental. Access to the properties
below varies considerably, so always
ensure that you contact the institution in
question to make arrangements and secure
bookings before visiting. Any houses that
are featured in this book but are not listed
below are strictly private and are not open
to the public. The owners politely request
that their privacy is respected at all times.

ASTLEY CASTLE – WITHERFORD WATSON MANN

Landmark Trust
1 Church Lane, Astley, Nuneaton,
Warwickshire, England, CV10 7QN
www.landmarktrust.org.uk/
search-and-book/properties/
astley-castle-4806/#Overview

BLACKWELL – M. H. BAILLIE SCOTT

Lakeland Arts
Blackwell, Bowness-on-Windermere,
Cumbria, England, LA23 3JT
lakelandarts.org.uk/blackwell/

THE COSMIC HOUSE – CHARLES JENCKS AND TERRY FARRELL

Jencks Foundation
19 Lansdowne Walk, London,
England, W11 3AH
www.jencksfoundation.org/
cosmic-house/visit

ELTHAM PALACE – SEELY & PAGET

English Heritage
Court Yard, Eltham, Greenwich,
London, England, SE9 5QE
www.english-heritage.org.uk/visit/places/
eltham-palace-and-gardens/

GODDARDS – EDWIN LUTYENS

Landmark Trust
Abinger Lane, Abinger Common,
Dorking, Surrey, England, RH5 6JH
www.landmarktrust.org.uk/search-and-
book/properties/goddards-8013/#Overview

HILL HOUSE – CHARLES RENNIE MACKINTOSH

National Trust for Scotland
Upper Colquhoun Street,
Helensburgh, Scotland, G84 9AJ
www.nts.org.uk/visit/places/the-hill-house

A HOUSE FOR ESSEX – GRAYSON PERRY AND FAT ARCHITECTURE

Living Architecture
Address on request [holiday rental]
www.living-architecture.co.uk/the-houses/
a-house-for-essex/overview/

LEUCHIE WALLED GARDEN HOUSE – JAMES DUNBAR-NASMITH

[Holiday rental]
Leuchie Walled Garden, North Berwick,
Scotland, EH39 5NT
www.leuchiewalledgarden.com

LIFE HOUSE – JOHN PAWSON

Living Architecture
Address on request [holiday rental]
www.living-architecture.co.uk/the-
houses/life-house/overview/

TURN END – PETER ALDINGTON

[Gardens only]
Turn End, Townside, Haddenham,
Buckinghamshire, England, HP17 8BG
www.turnend.org.uk

SECULAR RETREAT – PETER ZUMTHOR

Living Architecture
Address on request [holiday rental]
www.living-architecture.co.uk/the-
houses/a-secular-retreat/overview/

VOEWOOD – E. S. PRIOR

[Special events only]
www.voewood.com
Cromer Road, High Kelling,
Norfolk, England, NR25 6QS

ACKNOWLEDGMENTS

The authors would like to express their
sincere gratitude to all of the home owners,
guardians, architects and designers who
have assisted in the production of this
book. We would also like to express our
particular thanks to Alain de Botton, Faith
Bradbury & family, Hilary Carlisle, Carria
Kania, Karen McCartney, Danielle Miller &
family, Mark Robinson, Simon Willmoth
and the staff of RIBA Library along with
Lucas Dietrich, Fleur Jones, Yasmin Gapper,
Catherine Hooper, Anna Perotti, Jane
Cutter and the rest of the team at Thames
& Hudson.

INDEX

Page numbers in *italic* refer to the
illustrations and their captions

To Matthew

First published in the United Kingdom in 2023
by Thames & Hudson Ltd, 181A High Holborn,
London WC1V 7QX

First published in the United States of America
in 2023 by Thames & Hudson Inc., 500 Fifth
Avenue, New York, New York 10110

*The Iconic British House: Modern Architectural
Masterworks Since 1900* © 2023
Thames & Hudson Ltd, London

Text © 2023 Dominic Bradbury

Foreword © 2023 Alain de Botton

Photographs © 2023 Richard Powers

Designed by Anna Perotti
Project Editor: Catherine Hooper

British Library Cataloguing-in-Publication Data
A catalogue record for this book is available
from the British Library

Library of Congress Control Number 2023936162

ISBN 978-0-500-34374-6

Printed and bound in China by C&C Offset
Printing Co., Ltd.

Be the first to know about our new
releases, exclusive content and author
events by visiting
thamesandhudson.com
thamesandhudsonusa.com
thamesandhudson.com.au